STRAIGHT TO THE POINT

A Primer for
a Logical Introduction to Critical Thinking

David Lawrence Horne, Ph.D.

PEARSON

Custom
Publishing

Cover Art: *Probability*, by Angela Sciaraffa

Printed in the United States of America

10

ISBN 0-536-91893-7

2005440003

KC

Please visit our web site at *www.pearsoncustom.com*

PEARSON CUSTOM PUBLISHING
75 Arlington Street, Suite 300, Boston, MA 02116
A Pearson Education Company

TABLE OF CONTENTS

CRITICAL THINKING AND LOGIC

(OR, WHY BOTHER WITH THIS TEXT?)

Critical thinking, or evaluative reasoning, will be one of the most fundamental subject areas a student will study in college, no matter what specific major on which an individual student focuses. While thinking itself is usually described by such verbs as to weigh, ponder, fulminate, reflect, muse, deliberate, contemplate, cerebrate, cogitate, speculate, or consider, critical thinking as a distinctive process is essentially problem-solving, analysis, evaluative interpretation, making reasoned judgments, and making rational decisions. In each form of the process, one makes a choice or takes a primary point of view based on some amount of evidence connected to that choice or p.p.o.v. (primary point of view). The better (or stronger) the evidence and its relationship to the choice, the better (or stronger) will be the chance one has of making a thoughtful, measured, accurate and/or logical decision.

Of course, many of us are wedded to the daily practice of "feeling" our way through most decisions and choices: "I just know I'm right!" or "It's okay, I've got a good feeling about all this!" Not to discount the importance of that habit, but in the modern world it is rather crucial that one also learns how to choose a pathway, p.p.o.v., or action from several competing alternatives, based on the best available evidence or reasons to support such choice. That is critical thinking: the process of arriving at particular solutions, views or actions through identifying, organizing, evaluating and applying specific reasons that support or justify those solutions. To be sure, there is no one way to critically think or reason. There are numerous approaches and combinations of approaches which can incorporate hunches, intuition, tradition, stereotypes and even bigotry, along with tangible evidence. However, the primary distinction necessary is between reliance solely or primarily on "feelings" to arrive at a conclusion, stance or p.p.o.v.; and overall reliance on evaluating the tangible evidence available for such a conclusion. The latter involves the process called critical thinking while the former does not. Within that process are several layers and stages of evidence credibility; validity and soundness; organizing and prioritizing information; and the like. However, none of such internal differences within the critical thinking process should ever be confused with determining whether one's decision or judgments are arrived at through a reliance on "feelings," or a reliance on some form of tangible evidence. The former, simply put, is not critical thinking or critical reasoning and should not be viewed or judged by the rules of the critical thinking process. While emotional decision-making is, of course, thinking of a sort, it is not, and should not be mistaken for, critical reasoning or thinking.

Critical thinking does not necessarily mean thinking and decision-making that is always correct; instead, it simply means thinking and decision-making based on reasoned judgment and choices made based on the best available information at the time. Learning to think critically is the process of becoming familiar with the usage of patterns of reasoning or patterns of approaches toward problem solving. It is not formulaic or mechanical thinking whereby accessible information and data are always separated into distinct categories, and from those categories—and because the data is in those specific categories—decisions or judgments are made. Rather, critical thinking is a meticulous utilization of the patterns of problem solving approaches by adjusting or adapting one's approaches to the circumstances or the issue at hand. For example, the issue faced if you came home and found your house or apartment had been broken into, clothes and furniture strewn all over the place, and the noise of someone still rumbling through your bedroom desks and drawers, would be different and would require a different strategic response from you, than the issue raised if you went to your car to leave and found that it had a flat tire or that it was out of gas. In both situations you would have problems, but in each the circumstances would require specific critical thinking to match the issue or problem faced. What value is at stake? Is this situation life-threatening? If you do this or that, what are the costs or consequences? What chances are there for getting out of the situation? Do you need help? What neighborhood are you in? What time of day or night is it? . . . All of these, and more, are factors influencing your critical decision-making. That process is critical thinking.

One of the best types of critical thinking approaches—although certainly not the only one—is logic. Logic is the process of arriving at conclusions through argumentation based on the formal or informal organization of relevant evidence supportive of those conclusions. This text will focus on the introductory stages of learning to use logic—particularly deductive logic—to think critically in a modern world in which such skills are both necessary and critical.

Critical thinking is essentially problem-solving and analysis. To clearly distinguish between it and other types of thinking, especially "emotional" thinking, try the following activities. Students are reminded that it is the process of critically determining an approach to solving the problems listed, not whether they can find "right" answers, which is being studied here.

1. Determine how many people in your class were born in calendar months beginning with the letter J and in years whose last digit is 3.

2. Suppose you are shopping and you see an item you've wanted for a while on sale for, say, $5.95. The item looks damaged, there is a long line in the way of your getting to the item, and you have only 12 quarters, 13 dimes, 25 nickels and 4 cents left. Do you buy it?

3. Discuss whether America should or should not have gotten involved in the Iraq War. How did this country benefit? How did Americans benefit? How did you benefit? Are those the real issues?

4. What is the primary goal in life and what talents and assets do you have to achieve it?

5. If Fenster did it, then Laurie did too. If Laurie did, then so did Jack, Jill, and her dog Bill. If Jill did it, it's certain that Lil was nowhere near, and without Lil, Fenster does not move from his house or otherwise participate, so he couldn't have been involved. One thing is absolutely definite. Somebody did something, and if it wasn't one of them, then it was most certainly the other. Who did it?

6. Wally just called Sally an ugly witch who should always keep her broomstick handy to hide her face. She slapped him in response and let out a torrent of verbiage about his parentage. Was she correct in the way she responded? How would you respond were you involved in a similar situation?

7. You are lost. You got on the wrong bus or subway, or your car had a flat tire and ran out of gas in a neighborhood totally unfamiliar to you. It is getting dark. What do you do?

8. You get a letter in the mail informing you that you have won cash in a sweepstakes contest. All you have to do to claim your prize is to call a 900 number for $2.50/minute for approximately 15 minutes. Your friends say it is a rip-off. But none of them got a similar letter. What would you do?

CHAPTER ONE

WHAT IT IS: A LOGICAL DEFINITION

A. A BRIEF HISTORY OF LOGIC AND ITS USES

Logical reasoning, as an organized form of argumentation from given premises or evidence to a conclusion, was initially geometric reasoning. Geometry, plane and solid, was an invention and contribution to world civilization by the dynastic Egyptians, many of whom were Black Africans. It was geometry and stone masonry which allowed the building of the pyramids, from the first known example, the Step Pyramid of Sakkarra, approximately 2700 B.C.E., to the last, approximately 1100 B.C.E., in the Valley of the Kings of Karnak.

The Greeks, especially during the Hellenistic Period, further developed geometry and geometric reasoning (e.g. Euclidean and Pythagorean theorems), and also played a parlor game that eventually became formal logic, including syllogisms and symbols. The parlor game, recorded in Plato's works and first codified by Aristotle, presented logical reasoning as a set of yes-no questions and answers designed to lead to an irrefutable conclusion. The primary skill needed was the ability to frame suitable questions which would eventually lead, through a few or many steps, to the position advocated by the questioner. It was always the choice of questions that either sustained or that disrupted (when they weren't good questions) a line of logical reasoning.

Essentially, the game only involved two players who either chose a debating topic, or had it chosen for them by a group. One player—the questioner or inquisitor—took the yes position and tried to force the player taking the no position to switch sides in the interrogatives. If all of the no player's answers resulted in a forcible admission that yes was correct on the issue at hand, then the questioner won. If the questioner could not lead his opponent to such a concession, then he lost.

Below are two regular examples of how the game worked before Aristotle codified the rules.

1. SOCRATES WON THIS GAME IN TWENTY-FOUR MOVES OR QUESTIONS.

SOCRATES: Does not everyone see that knowledge alone is right?
MENO: I agree.
SOCRATES: Then, if virtue is knowledge, then virtue will be taught?
MENO: Certainly.

SOCRATES: Then, if virtue is of such a nature, it will be taught; and if not, then it won't?

MENO: Yes.

SOCRATES: And the next question is, is virtue really knowledge, or is it something else?

MENO: It is knowledge.

SOCRATES: Well, then, is it not true that, well, that which profits is wisdom—and virtue is profitable?

MENO: Of course.

SOCRATES: And thus, virtue is wisdom then?

MENO: That's true.

SOCRATES: But, if this is true, then the good are not by nature good?

MENO: Correct.

SOCRATES: But if the good are not by nature good, are they made good by instruction?

MENO: I concede. There is no other alternative, Socrates. On the supposition that virtue is knowledge, there can be no doubt that virtue is taught.

2. DIONYSODORUS: IF YOU WILL ANSWER MY QUESTIONS. AND YOU SAY YOU HAVE A DOG?

CRESPUS: Yes.

DIONYSODORUS: And he has puppies?

CRESPUS: Not by himself, but Yes.

DIONYSODORUS: And his offspring is his, not yours?

CRESPUS: But of course they are mine. He is mine.

DIONYSODORUS: Then he is a father, and he is yours, ergo, he is your father, and the puppies are your brothers. Let me ask you one more question. Do you beat this dog?

CRESPUS: But of course! He is a dog!

DIONYSODORUS: Then, I submit, that you beat your own father and your brothers!

From this basis, with Aristotle organizing the beginning and advanced rules into several manuals, the standard syllogism became the reference point for logic as a system of ordered thinking (e.g., All men are mortal. Socrates is a man. Therefore, Socrates is mortal.)

Syllogisms should have been seen afterwards as a series of questions intended to force someone to a predetermined conclusion, but quite frequently, through almost 2000 years, the syllogism has been seen as an argument in and of itself. Syllogisms, and formal logic itself, became rather detached from practical reality and instead became a series of rhetorical techniques to manipulate and cajole.

In the 19th Century, enter symbolic logic with its mathematical formulas and equations. Not only did the development of this dimension essentially "save" formal logic, the majority of logicians agree that this development also enhanced the credibility and evolution of informal, or content, logic.

In this text, Chapter VI will introduce the student to how syllogisms operate; informal logic, which is closer to everyday conversational situations, will be emphasized in Chapters 2, 4, and 5.

A. LOGIC DEFINED

Logic is the study of argumentation. Thinking is an overall process of connecting and synthesizing information, and logical thinking, as a corollary, is an interconnected series of learnable techniques and absorbed procedures. In this text, the relevant procedures to get students to learn how to think logically in progressively more complex ways will be emphasized. Students should pay attention to and grasp the fundamentals of logical thinking not as mere memorization of a concept or phrase here and there, but rather as a series of interconnected little processes to be learned and rationally applied.

Logical arguments are expressed as sequential statements or a combination of claims—generally oral or written—arranged and presented so that at least one of the statements or claims represents a conclusion or position taken, and the other statements, which are intended as support, represent evidence or premises for that conclusion. Squabbles, common quarrels, and disagreements based on mere assertions of opinions, beliefs, feelings, and wishes are generally not logical argumentation. Instead, logical argumentation is concerned with making claims or taking positions on issues backed up by evidence for or against such claims. Logic is the general art and science of argumentation, i.e., it is the study of making, weighing, and evaluating reasons for choices made and stances taken; and logic provides principles for discerning good (valid and sound) arguments from bad (invalid, fallacious, unsound) arguments.

As a written and oral usage of language, logic requires a skilled comfortability with linguistic activity. One's abilities in logical discourse increase directly with improvements in one's grammatical and compositional skills.

There are four principal categories of logic: deductive/inductive, and informal/formal. Within those broad categories are numerous branches of logic, including prepositional or clause logic; categorical logic; predicate logic; statistical and probability logic; modal logic; and others.

✳ DEDUCTIVE LOGIC, the primary focus of this text, can be defined traditionally as argumentation in which the truth of the premises, or evidence, conclusively establishes the truth of the conclusion. Another, perhaps more practical, way of conceptualizing deductive logic is that it is argumentation which is intended to make the conclusion an inescapable consequent of the relevant premises, i.e., the conclusion or p.p.o.v. taken is intended as a mandatory result of the associated evidence. When that intention is achieved, the deductive argument is valid; when it is not achieved, the argument is invalid.

✳ INDUCTIVE LOGIC, by contrast, is argumentation in which the conclusion is only made probable by the premises. In other words, inductive arguments are less definitive, by nature, than are deductive arguments. Induction aims at degrees of probability of the conclusion rather that at making the conclusion an inescapable consequent of the evidence. In a correct or valid deductive argument, accurate or true premises definitively establish the conclusion, while in a correct inductive argument, at best what can be achieved is that accurate or true premises provide highly probable support for the truth of the conclusion.

Only deductive arguments can be valid, and deductive arguments are correct deductive reasoning only when they are valid. Inductive arguments, when correct, are reliable, highly probable or good arguments, but never valid. Inductive arguments are most notably associated with statistical analysis, probability studies, and inferential reasoning. The latter essentially uses the amount and pattern of the available evidence to reason that a particular argument, event, or phenomenon in all probability is or is not true or will or will not occur.

Although inferential logic is usually associated most intimately with inductive logic, it is also regularly used in deduction, particularly when there are implied or unstated premises or conclusions presented as part of an argument. The essential point to remember in using an inferential approach is that the implied part of the argument has to be based on the information or evidence which has already been explicitly provided: one should not fabricate or wildly guess at items not already suggested by the evidence itself.

EXAMPLE

"Mary Alice knew that Spot would love the Krunchy Munchies Cereal she just bought, since all dogs love Krunchy Munchies." The unstated evidence within this argument is that Spot is a dog. How is that known? The given information links Spot with loving Krunchy Munchies, and it links all dogs with loving Krunchy Munchies. For Mary Alice to be certain that Spot too would love the cereal, then Spot would have to be in the category called dogs. Note that to determine the implied or missing evidence, the procedure was to stay "within the box" of evidence explicitly presented. Both Spot and dogs had already been mentioned in the evidence. All that was required was to link them relevantly together.

✳ INFORMAL LOGIC is argumentation which is dependent upon the relevant content and circumstances of the evidence presented to be valid. In other words, it is based on organizing, on making coherent, and on analyzing the evidence or the situation at hand so that when valid, the premises will lead mandatorily to the conclusion. A general definition of informal logic is that it is the study of argumentation in its real-world and everyday language context, based primarily on the RULE OF RELEVANCE (i.e., the evidence must be directly relevant to the conclusions drawn). Informal logic will be the first major category covered in this text. It will be contrasted with other practical situations regarding language used to persuade (See Chapter 3).

✳ FORMAL LOGIC, as distinct from informal, is argumentation based on the form or structure of what is presented. In formal logic, arguments are determined to be valid or invalid purely on whether their components fit the required forms, the actual content being besides the point. For example, there is the form called the logical syllogism which requires two premises and a conclusion composed of three terms, one term of which is used twice in the two premises, and the other two terms connected in the conclusion.

All apples are oranges.
All oranges are pears.
Therefore, all apples are pears.

if A=B
and B=C therefore
A=C

This example, whose content is obviously not "true" in the real-world sense, is completely valid according to formal logic because it simply fits the required syllogistic form. See Chapter 6 for a thorough introduction to Formal Logic.

C. PRIMARY USES OF LOGICAL ARGUMENTATION

There are different approaches used in logical argumentation. These approaches are in general motivated by the specific purpose or intention of the argument presented. The four primary uses of logical argumentation are (1) for persuasion, (2) for explanation, (3) for discovery analysis, and (4) for recording inferences.

✳ 1. The most typical and accepted function of logical argumentation is to convince, to persuade, even on occasion to compel, acceptance of a point of view. To be successful, such arguments generally need to be more than merely valid, and persuasive arguments run the range from simple and valid to complex, strong, and sound. (*Note:* An argument does not have to be either valid or sound to be persuasive or convincing.)

EXAMPLE 1

Listen to me carefully. This is mine. I selected it, bought and paid for it, brought it into my home and have gotten totally used to it. Private property laws are very straightforward in matters like these. Hands off ! Go and get your own! (*Note:* The logical issue here is whether "it" is mine or not. The logical claim is, "Yes, this is mine, not yours.")

EXAMPLE 2

The Educational Master Plan of any institution is its central long-term planning document. It identifies where the institution is intending to go educationally, why, with what constituencies, how, and when. It incorporates a process of program review and evaluation, of adapting the curricula toward a common reference point, and it accurately categorizes the distinct educational tracks available at the institution and articulates the transitional bridges between them. In short, the Educational Master Plan is an absolutely essential document for any institution serious about higher education, and this school does not have such a plan. It seems plain what kind of institution this is currently, and the issue is, how long will it remain so out of touch with the regular flow of the academic process? (The logical issue here is whether this school is serious about higher education. The logical persuasive claim is that no, this school is not serious about higher education as evidenced by its lack of an essential Educational Master Plan.)

✳ 2. A less recognized but also very typical usage of logical argumentation is to explain the why and how of a phenomenon, event, or activity. Explanatory arguments often satisfy our need to link what happened with motivations; causes with effects; actions with origins. Explanatory arguments teach and disseminate new information in an orderly manner.

EXAMPLE 1

Jimmy just stared at the mess in front of him: eggs, milk, butter, bread crumbs, all laying on the floor like a giant omelet someone started and then abandoned. Who had done such a thing? Then it occurred to Jimmy that maybe Alfonso was right: Jimmy did walk in his sleep!! This time maybe he'd walked straight to the refrigerator. Alfonso had sworn he'd seen Jimmy do that very thing last week !! (The logical issue here is whether Jimmy had been the one who had made the mess in the kitchen during a sleep-walking episode. The explanatory claim is that Jimmy had probably made the mess himself while sleep-walking.)

EXAMPLE 2

Bobby knew why he had $1.25 in change instead of the $2.50 he was supposed to have. The grocery clerk had thought that carton of milk on the counter was Bobby's and had charged him for it. And then, the milk was still put inside someone else's bags rather than Bobby's. Bobby figured he had gotten gypped twice in the same transaction. He hadn't kept a receipt, but now that he'd come to terms with what happened, he was determined to get his money back. (*Note:* The issue here is whether Bobby really knew (was right about) why he didn't have the amount of change he was supposed to have. The accompanying claim is that Bobby knew he did not have the correct change and he knew why. Lines 2–5 are evidence to support that claim.)

✳ 3. Arguments are also used, though less frequently, to ascertain the truth or accuracy of information. Such arguments are called discovery arguments and they generally render a given situation into a conditional argument in order to test whether some presented data can be relied upon or not.

EXAMPLE 1

Damon told Susan over and over again that he loved her and would do anything for her. Susan, of course, had heard it all before. "Show me," she said. "Walk up to Claire in my presence and tell her you're marrying me and that I'm the only woman for you. That I'm the woman of your dreams." Damon just stared at her a while, his jaw slacking. Finally he replied. "I can't do that." (*Note:* The argument is Susan's, not Damon's. Discovery arguments attempt to verify the accuracy of information presented by someone else. The logical issue is whether Damon loved Susan. Susan's claim is, "You say you love me, so show me! (Prove it!)" The evidence is, "If you do love me as you say you do, Damon, then you will do as I asked you. You, however, refuse to do it; therefore, you have shown me (proven to me) that you do not love me.")

EXAMPLE 2

NASA received with skepticism the Soviet invitation to send up a joint team of astronauts and cosmonauts. The invitation had even suggested a new partnership in sharing space "secrets" gained through the many years of the space race during the last 30 years or so since Sputnik. An uproar had been created when the board of directors read the correspondence in an open meeting, and the debate looked to be getting out of hand. Boydkins rapped a gavel for their attention and left this with the discussants: "Send them back a single sentence—'What are the design plans for the Solyuz Space Station—in detail?'" (*Note:* Boydkins captures the essence of the situation this way: The Soviets said they are ready to partner up with us. Okay, prove it!! If the Soviets are serious, they will provide the requested information. If they don't send the data, then we know they aren't serious, that this is just a ploy.)

✳ 4. A fourth and frequently frustrating utilization of arguments is for recording inferences (doing arguments with missing, implied parts). When deductively used, the inferential conclusion most often evolves from the relevant evidence implicitly and explicitly available to a reasonable conclusion, and when inductively used, inferences should lead to reliable and highly likely conclusions. Most frequently, inferences are reached by considering and eliminating other possibilities first. When, for example, students take Multiple Choice exams, and they do not know the answer to a test question but they can eliminate from five options the three or four least likely correct choices, then the answer chosen will either be the single remaining option or a selection from the remaining two. In such cases, students reason to what they consider to be correct from what they know (or believe) is not. That is an example of inferential logic. Here are a few more.

EXAMPLE 1

Bergen drank from the blue glass, gave a shudder and keeled over comatose. Myron, hesitating just long enough to observe what happened, gulped down the contents of the purple glass and, without waiting to savor the results, ran out of the cave into the sunlight, absolutely certain of his triumph. (*Note*: It is Myron's reasoning that we are concerned with here. His position was that there were only two options, one deadly and the other beneficial. When his companion collapsed after drinking from one option, the inferential conclusion had to be that the other was the beneficial one.)

EXAMPLE 2

John instantly knew he was no longer alone in the house. The door he'd closed tightly was now ajar. Even though he had not heard anyone come in, there was no wind blowing, and even if there had been, the door could only be opened by turning the latch in a certain way. The latch was too high for a dog or a child to reach, and no one could have left the premises without John seeing them first. (*Note:* The logical issue is whether John knew someone (or something) else was in the house with him. The inferential claim is that John was certain that someone (or something) taller than a dog or a child must have come inside the house and was still there even though John hadn't seen them.")

Identify the following as persuasive, explanatory, discovery, or inferential arguments. The types of arguments are not mutually exclusive (i.e., you can conclude a persuasive/explanatory or persuasive/inferential, etc. argument).

1. "You say you are the Chosen One, eh? Well, let's see! Toss him over the side, maties! Let's see him walk on water!"

2. "You better move it, buster! You see this big, black stick in my hand? It has only one useful purpose in this life: meeting heads. You want an introduction?"

3. Bolden looked poor, blind and pitiful in his rags, and in his generally bedraggled appearance. John, however, was a born skeptic. He decided to stand in front of the "Blind man" holding a twenty dollar bill out in plain sight for Bolden to take if he saw it.

4. "The stuff just blew up in my hands, Frank! Boom! I don't know what happened!!"

   "Well, did you read the instructions? Didn't they say not to mix part A with part B?"

   "Oh yeah. That's right. Sorry about blowing up your house, man. That's pretty messed up."

5. "If I move the T, it'll give me more space for the Q. If I have the Q, then, hot dog, I've got the P and the Z both. That'll only leave the Y, but the K is in the way of that. Hmmm. I've only got one move left and no time left to reconsider, so it's got to count big! So, bam! I did it! Gimme my 75 points!"

6. "I've only got 5 options here, and I know it can't be two of them; neither was ever discussed in class. Okay, so I've got three left, and one of those I know is clearly wrong. Of the two left, it must be B, since B is my favorite answer on a test."

7. He won the race not necessarily because he was better than everybody in the field. He won it because he had more heart than anybody else.

8. "You think you're that smart, huh? Well, who was the first U.S. president impeached, huh? Do you know that, Mr. Brainiac?"

9. "You need me and you know it. I'm the best one for you, the best you're gonna get, and the best you'll ever have! Lookahere! I've got brains, body, beauty, and I'm bad. So what's it gonna be?? The clock is ticking and my time ain't free."

10. "This is the best little compact on the road today. Go ahead, look at those comparison brochures! This baby gets the best mileage, it's got great resale value, and it looks like it was made with you in mind!"

11. If one and one equals two, and ten and twenty equal thirty, then without a doubt, Jack's whereabouts on Tuesday morning coupled with those mystery fingerprints clearly show that he couldn't have done it.

12. Whenever there's a full moon, the loonies strike up a tune and bay all night at the silvery balloons. Hmmm. We've got a bright full moon this night in June.

13. "Apparently, you cannot read, Mr. Jeeves! It says here plain as the ugly on your face that if you mix more than 2 parts salt with 3 quarts of that oxide, there'll be some unintended barbeque tonight!! So you got your skin fried! What did you expect, dummy?"

14. It is the beginning of the summer solstice and Polecat #2 is once again in his garden, enjoying the pretty colors and the dazzling smells. Such moments always reenergize him for everyday combat, and he'll need all the inspiration he can get for what's coming up next.

15. "If you want to know whether he's telling the truth, girl, just go ahead and get Suzy Taylor and bring her right in his face! Ask him in front of her. Then you'll know for sure! Make him prove it to you!"

CHAPTER TWO

LOGICAL ARGUMENTATION: A STEP-BY-STEP APPROACH

A. IDENTIFYING ARGUMENTS: STEP ONE

Statements and expressions either represent a logical argument, or they do not. There is no in-between with this. To determine whether any given statement or expressions do or do not represent an argument, use the process described below.

Note: Do not confuse whether you believe or accept the argument, whether you think the argument is a strong or weak one, or whether the content of the argument makes clear sense to you, with determining whether a given set of statements or claims does or does not represent an argument.

A PROCESS FOR IDENTIFYING ARGUMENTS FROM EVERYDAY SPEECH

1. A logical argument, whether simple or complex, always has the following ingredients: a primary point of view (p.p.o.v.), claim or conclusion (all equivalent), and evidence or premises to support it. The conclusion and premises can either be explicitly stated or written, or implicitly understood based on the information provided.

2. The p.p.o.v. or conclusion of any argument is the focus, the central theme or major stance taken in the argument. In other words, it is the central claim around which everything else in the argument revolves.

3. Most frequently, the p.p.o.v./claim/conclusion in the information presented will be a judgement (e.g., "That is wrong;" "You are the most inefficient of them all."), a choice (e.g., "This is the one, right here!"), a clear decision made ("I don't want you and I never did!"), or words of definitiveness (e.g., "He certainly knew the answer to that question!" "This is the only way to go;" "The red car had to be the best of the lot."). Pay attention to verbs and phrases such as "must," "have to," "should," "ought to," "could be the case," "was clearly the situation," etc., for strong clues for the p.p.o.v./claim.

4. To get to the p.p.o.v. or conclusion, choose one statement or claim which is part of the whole position presented and ask whether the remaining information answers what (in what way), why, or how in relationship to the statement chosen. If the other information does so answer why, what, or how, then the statement or claim chosen is the p.p.o.v./conclusion. If the remaining

information does not answer one of those questions, the statement chosen is not the p.p.o.v./conclusion, so choose another statement or claim within the information provided and repeat the process.

EXAMPLE

Socrates was older than Plato, while Plato was elder to Aristotle. Aristotle was thus the youngest of the three Greek philosophers. Choose the claim "Socrates was older than Plato" as the p.p.o.v/conclusion. In what way was he older? In the way that Plato was elder to Aristotle, and in the way that Aristotle was the youngest of the three? No. This makes no sense. Why is Socrates older than Plato? Because Plato is elder to Aristotle and Aristotle is thus the youngest of the three. Again, these statements do not answer the question why, so Socrates being older than Plato cannot be the p.p.o.v./claim. How is Socrates older than Plato? Again, the other statements provide no sensible answers to that question. The statement that "Socrates is older than Plato" thus cannot be the p.p.o.v./conclusion. Why was Aristotle the youngest? Because Socrates was older than Plato, and Plato was older than Aristotle. This made Socrates and Plato older than Aristotle, and thus Aristotle was the youngest of the three.

Use this process, questioning the parts of a claim/statement, to develop the skills of identifying whether or not a series of claims or statements represents an argument, and if so, what the conclusion and premises are for that argument. This process will identify the claim/p.p.o.v/conclusion from the information presented, if there is one there.

ANOTHER EXAMPLE

It's hot out here today, and this pizza is cold. Why is it hot here today? Because the pizza is cold? Nope. In what way is it hot, or how is it hot? In the way that the pizza is cold. Again, no. These make no sense here. Thus, "It's hot out here today" cannot be the claim/conclusion/p.p.o.v.

Do we stop there, given there's only one other possible claim listed? Absolutely not. "The pizza is cold." Why? Because it is hot out here today, right? Nope. That won't do. How or in what way is this pizza cold? Because it is hot out here today. Again, such an answer makes no sense. Thus, "This pizza is cold" cannot be the claim/conclusion/p.p.o.v. either.

Is there an implicit next step in information (i.e., when you add all of the information together, does it lead you one place?) that one can take given the combination of, "It's hot out here today" and "this pizza is cold?" Not really. There is no discernible connection between the two statements, so there is no next step to conclude from combining them. Thus, since neither statement alone or together provides evidence to support a third unstated claim, there is no logical argument here.

5. Commands used alone are not logical arguments. Thus, "Come here! Stop! Shut Up! Go home!" and the like, while they do communicate a viewpoint, cannot by themselves represent a real argument. Premises must be associated with such commands in order for them to be considered arguments.

EXAMPLE

I said to Shut up! I'm in charge here and what I say goes. You do what I say! (Argument: The p.p.o.v. is "You do what I say! Shut up!" Why? Because I'm in charge here, and what I say goes. Thus all the other information answers why for "You should do as I say," making that statement the claim/p.p.o.v./conclusion. The other information is evidence/premises which support the p.p.o.v./ conclusion.)

6. Interrogatives (Questions) must first be translated into declarative sentences in order for them to be considered as part of a logical argument or not.

EXAMPLE

Don't you feel stupid? Nobody else would stand up in my face and tell a boldfaced lie like that and then expect to get away with it! Procedure: First translate the question into a declarative statement ("You must feel stupid.") Then the p.p.o.v../conclusion = You must feel stupid. (Why?) Because nobody else (but a stupid person) would stand in my face and tell a boldfaced lie. And nobody else (but a stupid person) would expect to get away with it!

B. IDENTIFYING ARGUMENTS: STEP TWO: TWO SHORTER METHODS

1. Identify the purpose of the information being presented. Is it trying to persuade/convince you of something? Is it trying to sell you something? Interest you in something or someone? Is it trying to explain how some process works or how some situation got where it is? Is it trying to clarify the truth or credibility of some previous claim? Is it trying to do any of the above by implying and/or suggesting something rather than coming right out and telling you straightforwardly?

   a. If you can identify the purpose of what is being presented, look immediately for how the information tries to achieve that purpose. That will be your claim/p.p.o.v./conclusion.
   b. Identify the evidence/premises used to support that claim, if there is any such evidence presented. Don't make it up yourself, stick to what was presented in the information (fidelity, charity).

EXAMPLE

The blue bird certainly could not sing as well as the golden-throated warbler. Why, listen for yourself! The sound coming out of that blue bird crooner is sending those horses into a stampede and making the frogs over there leap for cover! (The purpose of this information is to persuade/convince us that the blue bird can not sing as well as the golden-throated warbler. This purpose is worked on by claiming outright that the blue bird simply isn't as good as the warbler, and the evidence used to support that persuasion is the admonition to listen for ourselves, and to look at the horses stampeding and the frogs leaping because of the sound of the blue bird trying to sing. From this purpose, we can identify what's there in the information and, since it is an argument, make it explicit.)

2. Identify the issue being discussed or written about in the information being presented. What is the most important idea or theme in the information being presented? What is most of the information "talking about"? What idea, concept, phrase is repeated the most? What, in other words, is the main point of the information being presented? Look for the subject and verb/predicate if that main point doesn't stand out immediately. Who or what is the information about, and what are they doing or having done to them? In the example above regarding the blue bird, what is the main point? The subject is clearly the blue bird, not the warbler, nor the horses nor the frogs. What is being said about the blue bird is a judgement that the blue bird cannot sing as well as the other bird. That is the claim/p.p.o.v.

   a. Put that main idea, concept, phrase, or point into a question: Can the blue bird sing as well as the golden-throated warbler? That is your logical issue.
   b. State the same sentence declaratively: The blue bird cannot sing as well as the warbler. That is your claim/p.p.o.v./conclusion.
   c. The other information in the presentation will usually be the evidence/premises for this claim, if such data is there.

Identify the following as arguments or not.

A.

1. Dorothy and Toto knew they were home in Kansas because they heard Auntie Em's high-pitched voice.
2. "Sit down and be quiet. We've got guests."
3. Dave was a cowboy alright. He had the outfit, the attitude, and the smell.
4. She screamed bloody murder at the sight of him.
5. "Stop, you fool! Stop the car! There's a train coming! Can't you see!???"
6. Bobby came home dirty and red-faced. His mother took one look at him and, without asking, concluded that he had fallen down in the street again, probably playing with his friends.
7. "I swear! If we lose one more time, I quit!"
8. "Put your hands up! This is a robbery! I need money and quick! You men empty your pockets. You women dump your purses!"
9. "Capitalism, my friend, is the only way. It's the way Nature intended. To the victor go the spoils and all that!"
   Response: "Bosh! If God had intended man to profit from exploiting one another, he'd have made us all card-sharks and gamblers!"
10. "I'm going left, since you told me to go right, and I know that you are always reliable if I simply do the opposite of what you say."

B.

1. The yellow bird never flies at night. That's why Donald was completely surprised at the brilliant flash of yellow feathers and the distinctive chirping sound of the yellow bird migrating in the moonlight.
2. "Yea, though I shall never walk this way again, lest I am tempted to sin; yet though I run through in hopes that my haste will neutralize my lust."
3. "When you add #5 and *79 you get (9*9), said Axel.
   "Where did you go to school, you moron? You can only get (7*6) out of that calculation," Briar shot back.
4. Everybody knows that Abraham Lincoln freed the slaves. After all, he was the greatest president this country ever had and he fought hard to preserve the union of states.
5. "I'm going to count to ten, then your behind belongs to me, you got that!!!?"
6. "Sollie, you are a fat, slouchy couch potato, you know that? Why don't you get your lard butt up from there and mow the lawn or find something to fix around here? Do something for a change except feed your face!"
7. The referees met in the middle of the field and made their decision quickly. Myron had traveled before he was fouled, so the Blue Crabs would get the ball out of bounds.
8. "I plead guilty, your honor, but with an explanation. I didn't do it. I swear I didn't."

9. If Egypt was Kemet before being "discovered" by the Greeks, and Kemet was the ancient name of the territory of the Wise Ones, and the Wise Ones in that time and place were mostly Black folk, then doesn't it stand to reason that the ancient Egyptians were a Black race of wise people before the Greeks polluted and diluted them?

10. "I invited, you accepted. I paid for it, now it's your turn. C'mon. You know the score, darling."

C.

1. My head hurts something terrible, so Justin must have been in this room before I got here.

2. "Nobody here is rich, Peter. Yet everybody here is wealthy beyond all words. They are old money, something I'm afraid that you wouldn't understand."

3. "C'mon Sal. Take a hit. Everybody else is doing it. What are you, some kinda square?"

4. The essence of the true religion is the belief that all men are brothers cut from the same fabric, and sisters painted with the same oils. Do you believe?

5. The Master Inquisitor knew how to get the real truth out of them all: those who screamed out the same story as the pain got more and more severe were the ones whose stories of truth he wrote down. The others said anything and everything in response to the twisting of the turnstile on their feet; so no, he couldn't believe that sort at all.

6. "Young man, you say you want to take my daughter out? Out where? You're walking and she certainly cannot drive my car. Are you on something?"

7. Dr. Davis was not granted tenure in the department. We all knew that. That's why we couldn't criticize the man for simply walking out of class one day never to return.

8. It's a known fact that slaves always want freedom; yet even when the word spread far and wide that the 13th amendment had legally destroyed their chains, many, maybe most of them, simply kept right on working on those southern plantations. Strange.

9. Those who do not heed the lessons of history are doomed to repeat the same mistakes. You, dear Jeffrey, are therefore doomed.

10. "If I had a trisket, I had a trasket; when I had money, I always had friends; and when I crossed over, I at least had peace of mind, yet no trisket, trasket, friends, or money. Maybe what I need is an agent."

11. "Look, a recession only lasts a year and change. This is going on 2½ years of economic turmoil and unemployment. I say this is now a bona fide Depression. A rose is a rose by any name, right?"

12. To find out what really happened that night, the reporter braved the bawdy street life to interview eyewitnesses neglected by the police and regular media. No one can say that this reporter didn't give it his best shot.

13. "You're an idiot, Barry."

    "And you're a fool, Mapes."

    "No, I'm Larry."

    "Fine, whatever your name is. You're still a fool."

14. "I want my MTV! Here. Here's $250. I want it now!"

C. PREMISE AND CONCLUSION INDICATORS: EXTENDING STEPS ONE AND TWO

Whenever the following words and phrases are used in logical arguments, they should be seen as important clues to determine which parts of the argument are premises and which part is the p.p.o.v./conclusion. *Note:* Remember, these indicators do not necessarily mean that the phrases associated with them are premises or conclusions; they are simply important clues useful in determining the composition of arguments. In informal logic, it is the context and meaning of the content that will ultimately determine what parts of the arguments are what.

Premise Indicators

Since
Because
For
Assuming that to be the case
Seeing that
Given that
In view of the fact that
Inasmuch as
Granted that
The reason is that
Based on the fact that
In light of
This being true because
As shown by the view that
As implied by the date that
It has been observed that
In support of this
The relevant data show that

Conclusion Indicators

Consequently
Therefore
Thus
So
Hence
Then
It follows that
Accordingly
The point of all this is
The implication here is
The result is
This being so
Which means that
As a result
We may conclude that
Which implies that
From which we can infer
This goes to show that
In conclusion
Finally
(As well as the verbs and phrases like "must," "have to," "should," "ought to," "certainly knew," "is clearly the case," etc.)

In real life, people rarely take time to label premise or conclusion indicators (also called inference indicators), nor do they often label the premises and conclusions in arguments heard or made. However, as students learning the art and skill of argumentation, it is useful to have certain efficient shorthand methods to identify the components of an argument to more expeditiously evaluate it. The following are relevant in this regard.

1. Underline or bracket premises and conclusions. Use a single line or bracket to identify premises and a double line or bracket to identify the p.p.o.v./conclusion.

EXAMPLE

Given that (a) <u>it's wrong to kill human beings</u>, it follows that (b) <u>Roe vs. Wade was wrongly decided since</u> (c) <u>it legalized the killing of baby human beings</u>.

2. The symbol .∴. is generally recognized in logic as the shorthand for Therefore or Thus.
3. To cut to the chase and make arguments explicit, i.e., to reduce the argument to its essentials of a p.p.o.v../conclusion and supporting premises, after underlining the component parts, list the premises alphabetically in sequential order (A., B., C., etc) and then the conclusion.

EXAMPLE

a. It's wrong to kill human beings.
b. Roe vs. Wade legalized the killing of baby human beings.
.∴. Roe vs. Wade was wrongly decided (*Note:* "Wrongly decided" is a comparative judgement and thus a clue for a claim/p.p.o.v./conclusion.)

4. Note that the order of occurrence in sentences has little to do with the logical sequence of labeling the premises and the p.p.o.v./conclusion. The latter may be at the beginning of the sentence, somewhere in the middle, near the end, or it may be implied rather than explicitly stated.

EXAMPLES

a. <u>That's just like Larry to be late</u>. <u>He's always getting to meetings after everyone else</u>, and <u>he's perpetually late for his classes too</u>.
b. <u>Because of your gaffe</u>, <u>I'm going to have to beg her forgiveness</u>. <u>She's too important a client to lose</u>.
c. When <u>the policeman asked Lonnie for his license and registration, pulled out his ticket book and started writing</u>, even before <u>he told Lonnie that he had clocked him at 70 mph</u>, <u>Lonnie knew what was coming next</u>.

Argument (a)
a. Larry's always getting to meetings after everyone else.
b. Larry's perpetually late for his classes.
.∴. It's just like Larry to be late. (*Note:* Why is it just like Larry to be late? Because he is regularly late to class and always late to meetings.)

Argument (b)
a. You screwed up. (You made a gaffe with a client.)
b. She is too important a client to lose.
.∴. I'm going to have to beg her forgiveness. (*Note:* The "going to have to" phrase represents words of definitiveness.)

Argument (c)

a. The policeman asked Lonnie for his license and registration.

b. The policeman started writing in his ticket book.

c. The policeman told Lonnie that he had clocked him going 70 mph.

.:. Lonnie knew (that he was probably going to get a ticket).

C. MAKING ARGUMENTS EXPLICIT: STEP TWO

As stated above, once an argument has been identified as such, it is useful to reduce it to its essentials: premises and a conclusion. Such reduction will help in properly and quickly evaluating and in critiquing the argument. Often there are "red herrings," or extraneous expressions and irrelevant items contained in or associated with an argument which simply get in the way when one is trying to understand, clarify or to evaluate an argument. Making an argument explicit, i.e., putting it into what is called Standard Form, eliminates all but the heart of the argument. To accomplish this, as noted in the previous section, list the argument's premises sequentially, numbering them, then either draw a line and under it write the p.p.o.v./conclusion or use the symbol .:. to represent the p.p.o.v./conclusion.

EXAMPLE

<u>You sold me some bad shoes, Joe</u>. And I'm not talking bad as in good, either. I'm talking bad as in bad! <u>Those brogans hurt my feet whenever I walked more than two blocks any one way, they soak up water like a camel,</u> and <u>they stink to high heaven</u>. My wife nearly fainted when I took those shoes off to go to bed last night.

a. The shoes you sold me make my feet hurt.

b. They soak up water.

c. They hold odors (They stink).

.:. You sold me bad shoes, Joe (and I don't mean good).

or

a. The shoes you sold me, Joe, make my feet hurt.

b. They soak up water.

c. <u>They hold odors (They stink)</u>.

You sold me some bad shoes, Joe (and I don't mean good).

ANOTHER EXAMPLE

Those greens you cooked made me sick, David. What'd you do, forget to wash them and then left them out all night after you had cooked them? It's too hot for that! Where's your mind?

a. You forgot to wash the greens. (Remember the previous section about interrogatives?)

b. After they were cooked, you left them out all night (in the heat).

c. I ate some of them (implied logical inference).

.:. Those greens you cooked made me sick.

In these two examples, the premises and conclusions are pretty straightforward. However, in many arguments the premises and conclusions are implied rather than stated forthrightly. In other words, either the premises or the conclusion itself will often be unstated, but still necessary to make the argument coherent. What is the process of making explicit the implicit parts of an argument (or making visible the invisible parts of the argument)?

FIRST, go through the argument identification process described earlier in the chapter. SECOND, based on that initial analysis, answer the following questions:

1. Are there premises presented for the p.p.o.v./conclusion that are overtly stated? (Or, put another way, are there reasons presented to support a point that is not overtly written or stated?)
2. If so, are those premises or reasons relevantly linked (i.e., do the premises identify items, ideas or information that are relevantly connected)?
3. Or, is the p.p.o.v./conclusion presented along with some evidence supporting it, but not enough evidence to make the conclusion mandatory?

If the answer to either of the three questions is yes, based on the information provided in that specific set of claims/statements, then there may be an implied argument or inferential argument present.

THIRD, in such a case, to determine the identity of the missing premise(s) or missing evidence, underline and label alphabetically the subject and object (and sometimes the predicate and qualifiers) present in the partial evidence provided.

EXAMPLE

Return to the Krunchy Munchies scenario of Chapter One:

(a)   (b)   (c)   (d)   (c)

Mary Alice knew that Spot would love Krunchy Munchies, since all dogs love Krunchy Munchies.

Here, there is a conclusion, a premise, and implied information which would connect the two more closely together.

a. All dogs love K.M. (d and c)
b. (Implied) Spot is Mary Alice's dog
.:. (a) Mary Alice knew that (b) Spot would love (c) K.M.

The provided evidence mentions all dogs (d) loving Krunchy Munchies (c). The conclusion mentions Spot (b) should love Krunchy Munchies (c). The missing evidence has to "Balance" the premises with what is in the conclusion (similar to balancing both sides of the equation in Algebra I). What the evidence mentions should be linked in the conclusion for the argument to be coherent and cogent (a.k.a., valid). In this case, the conclusion mentions Spot, but the given evidence does not. What remains to be done is to link dogs who love K.M. with Spot who also should love K.M. There is no evidence presented to link Mary Alice with being a dog, so Spot must be a dog in order for Mary Alice to know that Spot will love K.M. (as other dogs do).

FOURTH, if there is a missing or implicit conclusion, the same principle applies. The conclusion must connect the information provided by the premises. Do not bother "guessing" a conclusion that goes beyond the evidence presented. Stay within the box! (That is, stay within the range and scope of the circumstances, situation, and evidence presented. The same thing goes for "guessing" a missing premise. Stick to the information provided. Do not infer beyond the limits of that data.)

EXAMPLE

                    (a)   (b)   (c)   (d)
There was a fatal car accident last night at 5th and Main at 8:30 P.M. Jim always drove home that

                  (b)   (c)
way and passed 5th and Main religiously at around 8:30 P.M.

    a. There was a fatal auto accident at 8:30 P.M., 5th and Main (a, b, and c)
    b. Jim always drove (d) through 5th (b) and Main at around(c) 8:30 P.M. on the way (d, b, and c) home. (Implied) Jim was probably involved in that fatal accident. (a and d)

There are plenty of statements here, but none answers what (in what way), why, or how for the other. The statements are, however, related. They connect an auto accident, a specific time, and Jim's regular pattern and location of driving home. When you add them together they lead to several missing claim options (not one certain claim/conclusion, but an implied probable p.p.o.v.). To identify the missing p.p.o.v./conclusion, the task is to take similarities in the evidence provided and then pinpoint the differences that need to be merged. Here, the fatal accident (a) at 5th and Main (b) at 8:30 P.M. (c) is only mentioned in the first premise. The similarity is (b) and (c), which are both mentioned in each premise. Jim's driving that route on the way home consistently (d) is mentioned in the second premise, but not the first. Thus, (a) and (d) are the differences that have to be linked in the p.p.o.v./conclusion. Additionally, here one could not yet imply or assume that Jim was killed without more evidence than was provided (the data presented did not mention who died). Also, the use of "probably" is necessary here because the evidence provided does not say that Jim definitely took his same regular route home last night. Without more data, one cannot reliably imply or assume that he did. The logical issue is whether Jim was involved in that fatal accident. The claim/p.p.o.v. is that Jim was probably involved in that fatal auto accident last night at 5th and Main. *Note:* To have an argument, either part of the evidence (premises) or the conclusion can be implied or unstated. You cannot have an argument in which both the evidence and the conclusion are implied. To have an argument, there must be a reference point and the evidence to get you to that reference point. Absent both of these, there is no argument (i.e., whenever you have implied premises and an implied conclusion in the same set of claims/statements, you do not have an argument.)

In each of the following sections, identify the statements as arguments or not; if they are arguments, make them explicit. (Remember, implicit or inferential arguments are still first and foremost, arguments. Use the processes identified in this chapter.)

A.

1. If wishes were horses, then beggars would ride.
2. The economy improving? Not hardly. Just read the newspapers any day.
3. Big-time football is a joke in this city. Why, that sorry bunch of misfits couldn't score on a bunch of Pop Warner kids! They should be ashamed to call themselves a pro outfit!
4. Come home, and come home right not! I mean it! You hear me?
5. I'm sorry, Mrs. Lane, for your loss. Greener Pastures would like to serve you in this time of personal tragedy.
6. Chrysler backs them better, because Chrysler builds them better.
7. Buy new and improved Pride Soap Suds! The thinking woman's approach to the clothes game!
8. This is a dumb, stupid class! I'm not going back in there. Every time I show up, that so-called teacher throws a pop quiz on us like he's out of his mind or something, and I just get another flag. Forget that!
9. I'm not 49, you blind bat! Look at me! Does this look like the body of a 49-year-old? Well, answer me!
10. As soon as the gun sounded and everybody leaped out of the blocks, Antoine knew he had the race won. He had already beaten everybody entered in this race at least twice before, and he knew he'd gotten a great start!

B.

1. Triangle ABC is equiangular, as every equilateral triangle is. And since every triangle has only 180 degrees, each of ABC's interior angles must measure 60 degrees, right?
2. The only way to get there is to turn left, walk ten paces, turn right, then jump over the ditch. But could you do that? No! You had to try a short cut, so you turned right instead of left, and instead of jumping the frigging ditch, you fell smack into it.
3. I say the man is a bigamist! Listen, John is married and Gina is married too. That's all right. But Allison and Bill are also married, and not to each other. Allison is married to John and so is Gina. You see?
4. This is the way it is: You scratch my back, and I'll scratch yours.
5. His political career finally over, Lindy couldn't resist the temptation of endorsing someone he liked—in effect, naming his own successor. After all, wasn't he entitled?
6. I say that the question is right over wrong, good versus evil, Mom and Apple Pie against the devil and the deep blue sea. And you know that I'm right.
7. "Extremism is no vice in the defense of liberty," Polaris shouted. "America was built on such ideals and it has expanded beyond all expectations to where it is now because it never once backed away from that principle."

8. Separate education is inherently unequal education and must be prohibited by law.

9. Miles had to do something. His bank account was overdrawn, the credit vultures were circling round, and his wife was threatening to take the kids and leave. He had to figure out another brilliant move as he had always done in the past.

10. All of the round boxes in Silverlake are square, and all of the Silverlake boxes are also brown. Thus, Silverlake only has round brown boxes in squares.

C.

1. Thomas Jefferson must have been more than 57 years old when he died. In order to be president, Jefferson had to be older than 36, according to the law for all who serve in that office. The founding fathers thought this was important enough to preserve it in the U.S. Constitution. So when Jefferson did become president in 1801, he too had to toe the line about that age. Jefferson died in 1826, God rest his soul.

2. Miller is very tall and Piller is very wise. All tall men also want to be wise, and all wise men would enjoy being tall.

3. Whenever the warthog rooted his food and bent his snout, the cockatoo would take the opportunity to try doing what nature did not intend, singing, in a plainly irritating tone. So unpleasant was it that the elephant would immediately rush out of the foliage and trample thousands of fire ants in the process. The ants, once agitated, marched mercilessly into Cato Village and made life miserable for weeks on end. The warthog is at it again.

4. To love you is to adore you; to adore you is to need you; yet to need anybody is tantamount to slavery and dependency, a state I cannot abide. You must leave me this instant!

5. The U.S. Constitution says that only citizens can vote, and only certain citizens at that. I'm a certain citizen.

6. Ruth cannot have earned a degree in environmental planning because UCLA's graduate school doesn't offer a Ph.D in that.

DIAGRAMMING ARGUMENTS

An extension of the idea of reducing an argument to its essentials is diagramming or identifying a flow chart of an argument. Diagramming is extremely useful in trying to get a handle on a written argument and in writing one's own essays and arguments (and, incidentally, if one joins a debate team). Diagramming demonstrates what parts go where and are connected with what other parts to get to the conclusion or P.P.O.V.

There is no formula for diagramming, but there are several major principles one has to keep in mind in order to do diagramming properly.

1. Do not forget to look for the inference indicators as clues for premises and conclusions. Circle each inference indicator or bracket it, then number each premise and conclusion in the argument.

2. There are Independent Reasons which support a conclusion and there are also Dependent Reasons supporting a conclusion. The Independent premises (information which by itself can lead to the conclusion) can be connected straightforwardly to the conclusion by an arrow.

Dependent reasons (information, each piece of which, alone, cannot lead directly to the conclusion) must be connected or added together in order to, in sum, lead to the conclusion. Dependent premises are connected by plus (+) signs.

3. The plus signs (+) mean "in conjunction with" or "together with," and the arrows (↓) mean "is intended as evidence for" or "therefore."

EXAMPLE

We know <u>he is not a pleasant fellow</u>, since he's <u>regularly been obnoxious to Mrs. Allen</u>, and <u>he</u>
(1)
(2)

<u>just tripped poor Byron into the pool</u>. <u>He shouldn't be invited to any more of our parties</u>.
(3) (4)

This reads premise 2 together with 3 are intended as evidence for (or lead directly to) 1, and 1 is intended as evidence for 4.

4. Each arrow signifies a single step of reasoning. In the example above there are two steps indicated. Frequently, arguments have several steps.

5. There are basic and non-basic premises (also called primary and intermediate premises). Numbers with no arrows pointing towards them, only away from them, are basic premises (See 2 + 3 in the previous example), while numbers with arrows pointing both towards them and away from them are non-basic premises. (See premise #1 in previous example.) (Note also that 1, the first numbered premise in the previous example, is an intermediate conclusion which is then used as evidence or as a premise for a final conclusion.) The number at the bottom of the diagram with only arrows pointing towards it represents the final conclusion of the argument. In the example above, number 4 is the final conclusion.

6. When two phrases or statements are connected by an inference indicator, they should be underlined or bracketed as combined units within the argument, ignoring whether the phrases constitute complete grammatical sentences or not.

EXAMPLE

<u>I'm going home</u> because <u>you have hurt my feelings for the last time</u>. <u>I don't need this</u>, you hear me?

7. Also, some types of phrases should always be treated as complete units when diagramming, rather than to break them into component parts. These phrases are:

a. Either . . . Or (*Example:* Either sue me or sit down and shut up!)
b. If . . . Then (*Example:* If a frog had wings, then I guess he'd be a flying frog soaring in the heavens. Ugh!)
c. If and Only If (*Example:* If and only if I call you do you ever show up here again!)
d. Neither . . . Nor (*Example:* Neither rain, nor other adversity stopped Mr. Moonglow from digging in his garden.)
e. Only if (*Example:* Only if you're right can you come in here half wrong.)
f. Unless (*Example:* Unless you stop, I will simply leave.)
g. Until (*Example:* Until you are better, I won't bother you with details.
h. Before (*Example:* Before I catch this plane, can you give me a kiss?)

8. Arguments which contain several steps of reasoning which all support or lead to the same conclusion are called convergent arguments. Typically, diagrams of convergent arguments will have at least one number with several arrows pointing towards it.

EXAMPLE

Listen, (1) <u>I know someone else is there with you</u>, (2) <u>I can hear her talking in the background</u>, <u>you</u>
(3) <u>keep interrupting what you're saying to me to whisper to someone else</u>, and (4) <u>there's some strange</u>
(5) <u>hard rock on the radio at your place</u>, <u>which I know you hate with a passion and won't ordinarily</u>
<u>listen to</u>.

$$
\begin{array}{ccc}
\underline{2} & \underline{3} & \underline{4+5} \\
\downarrow & \downarrow & \downarrow \\
& 1 &
\end{array}
$$

Note: 2 and 3 are independent and basic, while 4 and 5 are dependent and basic.

9. One of the primary purposes of diagramming is to lay out the heart of an argument, thus avoiding information not relevant to that argument. (Essentially, this is the usual form of making an argument explicit). Make sure to leave such extraneous and "red herring" material out of your diagrams. Every component that does not contribute to the argument itself should not be contained within the diagram. Only include those components that do (including implicit components that are necessary).

EXAMPLE OF IMPLICIT ARGUMENT DIAGRAMMED

(1) <u>Monty is a Jesuit</u>, yet (2) <u>he is very tolerant of our Buddhist neighbors</u>.

(3)
(Implied conclusion) <u>Not all Jesuits are therefore intolerant of other religions</u>.

$$\frac{1 + 2}{}$$
$$\downarrow$$
$$3$$

Note: Whenever "yet" or "but" are used as premise or conclusion indicators, it should be remembered that both of them mandate a reverse of the preceding condition provided. Thus "She is going home, but I'm not" means "She is going home, and I'm not going home."

ANOTHER EXAMPLE

(1)   (2)
Paul is a Christian, which clearly shows that not all Christians are nice people.

(3)
(Implied Premise) Paul is not nice.

$$\frac{1 + 3}{}$$
$$\downarrow$$
$$2$$

Note: At this point, students should be able to do simple implicit arguments as provided in the examples above. Remember to be Charitable when composing an implicit conclusion or premise (i.e., give the argument the benefit of the doubt); show Fidelity to the argument (i.e., make sure you are faithful to the information provided—do not go beyond the boundaries of the information you are given in the argument in order to ferret out the missing conclusion or premise); and maintain Balance in the argument (e.g., what the premises "talk about" is what the conclusion results in, and vice versa).

REFERENCE EXAMPLES OF A SERIES OF DIAGRAMS, FROM SIMPLE TO RELATIVELY COMPLEX

(1)   (2)   (3)
a. She didn't know that my wallet was gone, since nobody told her and she wasn't there when it

(2)   (4)   (5)
was taken. Since she didn't know, there is nothing she could have done about it. She bears no

(6)
guilt in this tragedy. My wallet's gone . . . stolen . . . and that's that.

b. <u>If he comes home, I'm leaving</u>, and <u>if he calls, I'll not speak to him</u>. Either way, <u>I'm not interested in dealing with him at all</u>. <u>He makes me sick</u>.

(1) ... (2)

(3) ... (4)

$$\frac{1+2}{\downarrow}$$
$$4$$
$$\downarrow$$
$$3$$

c. <u>Jan knew her before she started to work</u>, since <u>they went to college together</u>. Since <u>Peter only met her when she got the job here</u>, <u>it's obvious who's known her longer: Jan!</u>

(1) ... (2)

(3) ... (4)

$$2$$
$$\downarrow$$
$$1+3$$
$$\downarrow$$
$$4$$

d. Look, sir, I'm sorry but <u>it says right here that this check is void unless cashed within 30 days</u>. <u>We can't cash it here</u>. <u>Today is Friday, March 15</u>, and <u>your check was issued on January 15</u>. It's void, sir. <u>We can't help you</u> . . . Next!

(1)

(2) ... (3) ... (4)

(5) ... (2)

$$1+3+4$$
$$\downarrow$$
$$5$$
$$\downarrow$$
$$2$$

e. <u>Sherry must have been home by 7:30 P.M. last night</u>. <u>I heard the phone answered in her apartment right past then</u>. <u>I saw her lights come on about that time</u>, and <u>I saw her standing in front of the window again right when the 7:00 news was going off</u> and <u>it's only a half-hour show</u>. (*Can you do the correct diagram here?*)

f. The Spartans basketball team will probably lose in the championship game for two very ⁽¹⁾ distinct reasons: their two best players won't play and everybody else is simply too tired to ⁽²⁾ ⁽³⁾ pull off the upset. If they do lose, the coach will probably get fired, although not just because ⁽¹⁾ ⁽⁴⁾ of that. He's been at the center of a grade inflation scandal all year and this school simply does ⁽⁵⁾ ⁽⁶⁾ not allow that kind of bad publicity. So if the team loses, it'll make easing him out easier. ⁽⁴⁾

(Implied: The coach will probably be fired.) ⁽⁴⁾

$$\underline{2 + 3}$$
$$\downarrow$$
$$\underline{1 + 5 + 6}$$
$$\downarrow$$
$$4$$

D. ARGUMENT VALIDITY AND SOUNDNESS: STEP THREE

Once arguments are identified and explicated, the next important stage is to preliminarily evaluate them, i.e., to determine whether they are valid, and if valid, whether they are sound. Logically validity can be defined basically two ways: (1) As an argument whose conclusion cannot be false when its premises are true, and (2) more practically, it is an argument whose conclusion is mandated by the direct relevance of its premises. In other words, an argument is logically valid when its conclusion necessarily follows from the specific premises to which it is directly and relevantly linked. (The claim/p.p.o.v./conclusion is a certainty based on the evidence used.)

EXAMPLE (FROM PREVIOUS SECTION, WITH ADDITIONAL DATA INPUT)

a. You forgot to wash the greens before you cooked them.
b. And after they were cooked, you left them out all night (in the heat).
c. Because of this, the greens went bad. (Implied)
d. Afterwards, I ate the greens and nothing else all day and I got sick.
∴ Those greens you cooked made me sick.

This is a valid argument because it adheres to the definition given above: the conclusion follows mandatorily from the premises.

ANOTHER EXAMPLE

That green is blue, since all greens are blue, and it's certainly very green!

> a. All greens are blue.
> b. That one is certainly very green
> ∴ That green is blue.

Logically validity, as you can see from example two, does not necessarily mean that the argument's content always has to make common sense, and it certainly does not mean that either the premises or the p.p.o.v. have to be true. More of this will be discussed under formal logic. The point here is that the evidence provided must lead inexorably to the specific conclusion for an argument to be valid. The measurement then for validity is straightforward. Both of the following questions must be answered and answered in the affirmative: (1) Is the evidence (the premises) provided or inferred directly relevant to the p.p.o.v./conclusion? And, (2) Is the p.p.o.v./conclusion a certainty, given the evidence provided and/or inferred? When both questions are answered by yes, the argument under scrutiny is valid.

Logical soundness is another matter. Although validity is the meat and potatoes of deductive logic, good argumentation aims at more than validity, it aims also at soundness, which is deductive logic's gravy. It is what is commonly known as a steel-trap argument. To be sound, an argument first has to be valid, then its premises must either be verified as true or be verifiable. If neither, then the argument cannot be sound (even if it is valid, and validity, of course, is required before an argument can be sound). A sound argument is a logically tight argument that does not violate the rules of argumentation, and that presents evidence and a conclusion in a cogent, compressed, organized manner. Sound arguments (particularly strong and compelling sound arguments) are the most credible in logic and discourse, and they are the ultimate aim of argument presentations.

However, deductive logic itself is generally defined as the study of logical validity. Soundness is essentially the cake icing; validity is the basic cake.

In the previous two examples, the argument on greens is valid and Contingently Sound, since the premises and the conclusion are all verifiable, but not yet verified. (The argument is Sound only when the particular sequence of events occurred just as stated and the greens were in fact the only food the arguer had before getting sick; otherwise it is Valid but Unsound.) The second example is valid but unsound, since it is not either verified or verifiable that all greens are blue. It is most often easier to prove logical unsoundness than it is to prove soundness, given the fact that evidence verifiability is frequently in dispute. In general, evidence which contradicts the laws of nature; evidence based on an appeal to morality, emotion or aesthetics; evidence based exclusively on absolutes; and evidence which contradicts known facts, will not constitute a sound argument. Thus, religious arguments; moral/ethical arguments; arguments comparing the beauty or value of paintings, music, theater pieces or other artistic productions; arguments such as "All men are dogs;" "All Black folk love to party;" or "All whites are racists;" etc., will not generally be sound arguments under virtually any circumstances. The very rare exceptions will not change the rule.

In the items below, when they are arguments, make them explicit (this includes implicit arguments), then identify whether they are valid and sound.

1. Mr. Lemon's puzzling illness was finally diagnosed as terminal cancer, giving him but a few months to live, if the doctors are correct. They still have not told him yet and must find a gentle but firm way of conveying this news to him so that he can arrange for his domestic, business, and financial affairs to be handled.

2. Anyone who can dance like that certainly can't be a passive-aggressive personality, and Antonio absolutely is not one.

3. Everything that attracts and holds my attention in this life seems to be dangerous, criminal, or sinful. You, my pretty, are assuredly neither dangerous for me nor criminal.

4. I heard some fool in the park yell at me: America—love it or leave it! Well, I'm not going anywhere.

5. The way I see it, if I'm now old enough to wear the uniform and defend the country, putting my own young life at stake, then I should be able to buy myself a little 6-pack when I want one, and I want one right now!

6. Who asked you to speak for me? I sure didn't. Don't tell me about dying from smoking. If I want to smoke, I'll smoke. If I want to try bungee jumping, then I'll do that. Don't presume to state what you think is good for me. I'm fully capable of deciding on my own, thank you.

7. Jess bet Walt that he could drink Walt under the table. Maybe so, but it's Jess who's now laying out like a pickled whale on the floor.

8. "Whoever done the deed," cackled Train Man, "has got a mighty good shooting eye, 'cause they hit Ole Oscar dead center of his forehead from 500 yards away with a .30 odd special deer rifle. Ain't nobody round here can do that but Grayson and Benthorne. So it was definitely Benthorne who done it and in cold blood too."

9. The strike is on at the crack of dawn if the band members march on in their blue carry-ons. That crowd coming towards me at 'fo day in the mornin' playing their instruments loudly sure looks pretty blue to me today. Sure does.

10. No African American has ever been elected to the U.S. presidency, and none ever will. And that's the honest-to-God truth.

11. If the right to vote is the quintessential qualification for citizenship, then I guess women were merely residents and not real citizens of this country until the 1920's, since they certainly didn't have that qualification.

12. If a man is very nice and charming, he can meet nice people wherever he goes and he can have a lot of friends. Wilbur is a man all right, but he has hardly any friends, so he must not be a nice man.

13. God is dead, and so are you. But then again, who's reading this then?

14. Students are simply not good judges of character, or else why would so many of them flunk out of Prof. Drucker's class?

15. You want to know my opinion of you? Hmmmm. Well, my mother, whom I always obeyed, told me to remember to say something nice about everyone or else just shut up. That's all I'm saying.

16. The American, Norman Mailer, will not win the Nobel Prize for literature this year, since an American won it last year.

17. Omigosh! The temperature hit 110 degrees in the shade in Needles, California, yesterday, according to the CNN reporters.

18. He's young, lean, mean, and a brute in the ring. I want him!

19. A fool and his possessions are always quickly separated. That's why Harold is living in the streets nowadays.

20. I only meant to give you love and tenderness. The hurt was accidental. So was the broken arm you got. Sorry about the concussion too. I only meant to love you.

21. I am the great Bambola. I sing. I swing. I carouse. I bring happiness. I am the one and only, so get off of my platform, buddy!

22. This is the way it is. Uhh . . . like I said, this is . . . Leave me alone! No! I said no, I don't want to and don't intend to! Back off or die!

23. Hallelujah Hawkins wasn't sure this was the right choice to make so she licked her thumb, held it up to the air to see whether it was hot or cold, closed her eyes, and hoped for the best. The ribbon she drew from the basket was the one worth $50,000.

24. I did it because I could do it and I could do it because I'm bad. So there!

CHAPTER THREE

ELEMENTS OF NONARGUMENT PERSUASION

Having learned what an argument is and is not, it is rather important to become acquainted with every-day conversational devices that often masquerade as logical reasoning. They are generally called Slanters and Teasers (S & T, or Hidden Persuaders) since they mainly act as suggestions or as emotional influences for accepting or rejecting a point of view. In fact, they do not provide credible reasons or evidence for accepting or rejecting a claim, although in ordinary conversation they often "feel" like they do.

Slanters and Teasers most often manipulate positive or negative opinions in listeners or readers; or they mislead persons into uncritical thinking and emotional responses. In effect, they prejudice issues by appealing to suggestive, emotional, or strongly fearful language. Though sometimes they appear to be actual logical arguments to the untrained eye and ear, Slanters and Teasers are not arguments. At best, they are pseudo-arguments—substitutes for real reasoning and critical evaluations. They are mere hints, urges, and teasings, and should be recognized as such. Although such devices do have their place within clear and concise writing and speaking, as colorful, creative language, their predominant usage as semantic trickery makes them especially seductive to students of introductory logic.

The following list of Slanters and Teasers is not exhaustive, but it does contain many of the most common ones.

A. EUPHEMISMS

These are words or phrases meant to disguise or minimize some unpleasantness, an offensive activity, or a bad situation. Euphemisms are most frequently used to deceive persons into considering or accepting a point of view, although they can certainly be used for constructive purposes also. In general, they are nice ways to refer to bad things. Examples include a military report of "significant collateral damage in an area" (heavy civilian and non-military casualties) or the Department of Defense just announcing the development of a "property-friendly exploding unit" (a bomb which kills people but spares the buildings occupied by those people). Other examples are, "Mr. Parker, I'm happy to tell you that you've just been selected for our new employee redeployment and outplacement program" (you've been fired); "Yes, I have a job. I'm a cash transactions specialist" (a hold-up man); or "My client, admittedly, has a little sexual problem that needs treatment" (he's a rapist or a child molester).

Euphemisms color the truth or sugarcoat a bitter pill. They usually cause trouble when their inventive names, labels, or phrases for distasteful subjects attempt to mislead, manipulate, or fool people into accepting the distasteful subject as something good. Clues indicating the presence of a Euphemism include the usage of any words or phrases to describe something bad, scary, horrifying, or amoral as something nice, cuddly, soft, easy, etc., such as "a loved one has passed on to glory" instead of "she just died."

B. DYSPHEMISMS

These are the opposite of Euphemisms. They are words or phrases which attempt to minimize the positiveness of a subject, to change the positive to a negative, or to make what is already negative even more negative. Dysphemisms are generally intended to leave a bad taste about a topic, person, situation or other subject in the mind of a listener or reader. Examples include, (a) "This would have been a good class if the teacher hadn't been so stupid." (b) "Look at that fat Santa Claus!" (c) "Yo! You with the big wart on your face!" (d) "Get out, go home or to one of the other nasty places you hang out in!" In the current vernacular of student slang, a Dysphemism is a "diss". i.e., a downgrading of a person, thing, or subject. It makes candy bitter or at least tries to make it leave a sour aftertaste. Clues for the presence of a Dysphemism include the usage of words or phrases (mainly adjectives and nouns) which downgrade something or someone which has a positive association, or which make a bad situation or description even worse than it already is.

C. PERSUASIVE COMPARISONS

These are words and phrases that liken a person or situation to another person or situation, with the original subject of the comparison already having either a positive or a negative public association. The aim is to create a persuasive impression or attitude about the person or situation being compared. Examples include, (a) "You drive like a plumb fool!" (b) "You're pretty short, aren't you. Just like a little ugly troll under the bridge." (c) "Just like a nasty buzzard, you always show up when you think you can get something for nothing." (d) "Like a scared rabbit, at the first sign of trouble, you turn tail and run." (e) "As putrid as that green slime is, that's how I see you, buddy!" (f) "You might as well be a deer in headlights for all the insight you've provided."

Clues for the presence of a Persuasive Comparison are phrases with "Like" or "Just like," "Just as," "more this than that," etc.

D. PERSUASIVE EXPLANATIONS

These are words or phrases that attempt to tell "why" some occurrence, activity, attitude or "fact" happened or is happening a certain way. The "why" is always unsubstantiated opinion and it is usually focused on an unflattering description of someone's personality, motivation, state of mind, or the like as an "explanation" of "how" or "why" something occurred. Examples include, (a) "We lost the stupid game on account of John's stupid play." (b) "Sure, I fell down and broke my leg all right. Know why? Because you didn't stop me, you s.o.b., that's why!" (c) "Know why I'm bald? Because your constant foolishness made my hair fall out!" (d) "See here! See here! They're taking me to jail. Why did you make me beat you up like that? Huh?? Why!!?" Clues to indicate the use of a persuasive explanation include words used as "reasons" for something occurring that are merely one's unsupported beliefs or opinion.

E. PERSUASIVE DEFINITIONS

These are words or phrases which mix positive or negative prejudices into an identification of a person or thing in an attempt to influence a listener's or reader's view about that person or thing. Most commonly, this is the verb to be, or some derivation, and the statements act as "arguments by assertion," or "arguments by pronouncement." Examples include, (a) "That's a bonehead move. It certainly fits your intelligence." (b) "To the British, Mr. George Washington was far from a freedom fighter. He was purely and simply, an anti-government terrorist whom they were rightfully told to shoot on sight!" (c) "Civil disturbance in a pig's eye . . . that was a Black riot of Negro and Mexican looters frightening the hell out of decent people!" Other examples include, (d) "Margo's a really beautiful and classy lady, you know!" "Yeah, maybe to you, but to me she looks like a 'ho.'" (e) "Look, there's one of those homeless persons trying to make a little money by pumping gas! Whatdya say we help him with some coins?" "Homeless??!! That guy's a dope addict hustling dimes and quarters to get the price of a hit. Don't be a sucker!!"

Regarding clues indicating the use of Persuasive Definitions, most P.D.'s, as mentioned earlier, use some variation of the verb to be, e.g., "I know that abortion is the murder of an unborn child," or "You look fine, but it's obvious that you must be an insane fool to try that around here!"

F. STEREOTYPES

These are words or phrases which generalize attitudes or actions to implicate a whole class or group of people. Examples include, (a) "You talking about violence? Then you're talking about Black people!!" (b) "Find me a red-headed, no talking, raunchy bum, and I'll show you an un-American immigrant trying to con somebody." (c) "Women are too emotional to make hard-headed business decisions, Paul, and you know it!"

Clues indicating the use of a stereotype include lumping all of anything or anybody into one behavioral category. The Slanters and Teasers, A-F, represent the type of Slanters and Teasers which depend on emotional manipulation, in the main, to be effective (although both Euphemisms and Dysphemisms depend as much on verbal trickery as on evoking emotional responses). The following Slanters and Teasers base their influence primarily on semantic manipulation.

G. INNUENDOES

These are words or phrases that through suggestive statements, insinuate negative or insulting information about a person or thing. Examples include, (a) "Sure, Harvey hardly ever lies." (b) "Well, she's very good at her work, for the most part." (c) "Is that what you're going to wear? Nice. Very colorful. Very . . . Uh, why don't we take separate cars, alright?" (d) (Teacher passing an F paper back to a student) "Really distinctive work, Mr. Purdy. Keep it up. This is just the kind of work I'm expecting from you."

Clues indicating the use of Innuendo include subtle putdowns, implicit insults, and misdirected praise and wisecracks saying one thing but implying or suggesting something else. It is what some refer to as "witty," sarcastic, "biting wit" or being a "smart-ass." These insults tend to sneak up on you.

H. WEASELERS

These are words or phrases which ask misleading questions, or blunt direct statements by using words like "maybe," "perhaps," or "possibly" to make a point. The aim is to say or write something without being held accountable for the words used. Examples include, (a) "Some people think Allen is definitely guilty." (How many is some? 98 out of 100 could think one way, 2 can be the some who think another way); (b) "Most faculty questioned gave support for the president/superintendent." (How many were questioned? Three? Four? If 2 out of 3, or 3 of the 4, all of whom may be friends of the president, support her, then the statement cannot be criticized the way it is made, and it sounds much more credible than it actually is.); (c) "Perhaps you really are the thief they're looking for?" (d) "Maybe this isn't the right thing to do or the person to do it with, but that's okay." (e) "You know, it's quite possible that we are not alone. Earth may not be the only inhabited planet." (f) We're not sure, but in all likelihood, men have always been in charge of things."

As mentioned above, clues for the use of Weaselers include words like perhaps, possibly, maybe, and some (although be careful not to automatically make the assumption that a Weaseler has been used simply because you read or hear these words used in a claim or statement), and the use of elementary statistics (3 out of 4, etc.) to recommend a product.

I. DOWNPLAYERS

These are words or phrases which give a compliment or words of praise then take it away, thus undermining the significance of another's accomplishment or achievement. Examples, include, (a) "You got a mere B on the test, but I really scored!" (What did "I" score?); (b) "This so-called doctor of something or other just told me to quit smoking or I'll die!" (c) "Sure he won, but so what? I wasn't even trying!" (d) "You know, you're sort of pretty, in spite of that giant pimple all along the side of your face."

Clues for the use of Downplayers include the mention of some achievement or distinction associated with the words "so-called;" "mere" or "merely"; "but" or "nevertheless." Again, a caution: Don't automatically assume a Downplayer just because you see or hear these words in a claim. Pay attention to the circumstances of use.

J. PROOF SURROGATE

These are words or phrases that hint and suggest evidence or support for a claim without really providing any for it. Typically, students confuse statistical Weaselers with Proof Surrogates, particularly such phrases as "a lot of people," and "most people feel that." Proof Surrogates are usually more specific than Weaselers. For instance, a statistical Weaseler will generally be of the type, "the average citizen knows that," or "3 out of 4 doctors feel that," etc. A Proof Surrogate would be, "the average citizen surveyed would tell you that," or "3 out of 4 doctors contacted would argue that . . ." Note the difference in verb usage—surveyed and contacted. Typical examples of Proof Surrogates include, (a) "It's obvious that I'm right! Any fool can see that!" (b) "Many recent studies have shown that this pesticide is dangerous." (c) "Informed sources I've contacted have told me that the stock market will crash in exactly 3 days!" (d) "Everybody who is anybody knows that Preston is the best pianist around!" (e) "It is perfectly clear which path will lead us home!" (f) "Any good Christian asked would know what to do." (g) "3 out of 4 dentists surveyed recommend Ipana toothpaste to their patients."

Clues for the use of Proof Surrogate include, "It's perfectly clear to everyone that ...," "It's obvious that . . .," "Informed sources say that . . .," "Studies show that . . .," "Everybody says that . . .," "A high percentage of people polled say that," "Many people surveyed feel that," etc.

K. HYPERBOLE

These are words or phrases making exaggerated and extravagant claims, usually far out of context or credibility for the circumstances mentioned. Examples include, (a) "She is absolutely the most beautiful woman in history." (b) "You are the most ignorant person alive on the planet!" (c) "John Coltrane was by far the best sax player who ever lived and who will ever live!" (d) "You won't give me even one stinking dollar to get some food??!! You are a racist dog who should be fed to the sharks!"

Identify the dominant Slanters and Teasers in each of the following items. There may be more than one S & T in some items.

A.

1. Perhaps the troll lived after all. Or maybe Bobby just saw a big roach. I know for certain that Bobby wouldn't just lie to me out of the blue.
2. You think maybe she actually did him in? She's a crafty one and I wouldn't put it past her. No siree!
3. The car is a total lemon. Shoot it and put it out of its misery and out of my life.
4. University tests consistently show that Skinny-Fast Diet works wonders in just days. Want to melt away your unwanted body puffs and dimples? Want to feel the grace of the gazelle replace the thundering thighs of your modern life? Then try Skinny-Fast Diet. You won't regret it.
5. Like the jackrabbit he is, he simply ran at the first whiff of danger.
6. It should be perfectly clear that this is a better choice for you, Mrs. Davis!
7. In history class today, we learned how the 19th century U.S. government consistently resettled Indians from Georgia and Florida to Oklahoma.
8. John is the best catch she ever made, and the only one too.
9. Peter's got a negative cash flow problem and Violet's in the family way again. They won't be joining us this year, I'm afraid.
10. Although it's a bad day, it's better than not having any day at all.
11. She should really be an Olympian one day, in her own mind.
12. Mariam won the championship again this year, but even she knows that she didn't deserve it.
13. Boggs stole a look and sized up the situation. He then snuck up on poor Mr. Freeze and mur-
    ___ an with one stealthy blow.
    ___ ou are the worst thing to ever happen to me. You are just an absolute jerk! The worst
    ___ le life comes Grace, with all her bumbling charm.

1. So what if his name's not listed in the college catalogue. That doesn't necessarily mean that he doesn't teach there anymore. Maybe he's on sabbatical or something. Or maybe he's an administrator! Yeah.
2. Could it be that Maxey Lode has found religion now that his airline is actually profitable again? He's the one who used to advocate a complete governmental takeover of the industry. Now look at him! Flying high and espousing the virtues of deregulation!
3. Hey, Mr. Potato Head! You're nobody's dreamboat, so stop harassing people in here! If you want a girlfriend, then go down to the zoo with your own kind!
4. Buddy, look here! This ain't the wild, wild West, and you're not Wyatt Earp. Get back.

5. You want to make an honest woman of me? Is that what this pitiful charade has been about? Well, let me help you: No, I will not marry you, not now, not tomorrow, and not a zillion years from now! Be gone, poot-butt! And stay away!

6. "Tony, let's embrace this fine automobile as true gentlemen of leisure. No key? No problem. I remembered to bring along my zippy Slim Jim and we'll be out of here like quicksilver in 20 seconds or so, okay? After all, we do not have other appointments on our calendars today."

7. Even though Mrs. Jones had seen countless slobs like Jerry, she submits that he was a true artist of dilapidation and therefore deserved her best condescending air.

8. If the students I've surveyed were telling the truth, he's a competent, if not charismatic, teacher.

9. We all know about Mark, Mary, so you may as well tell us the whole story and free your conscience.

10. You look like Howdy Doody and act like Dagwood Bumstead. You are a piece of work, indeed!

11. Fire the cannons! Loose the bombs! My mother-in-law's at the door and she's packing irritation, loud cackling, and nothing but hard times!

12. You want to know what I think? Sure you do! And I'm the man in the moon!

13. C'mon baby, my life depends on this. Gimme all your pocket change!! I've got a great video game score going here and I don't want to quit!

14. Look at Pete. Sitting there holding his cards like a Buddha in heat. I know him. He's a pure fake. He'll raise the bet, get called and fold like he always does. He's got no heart! He may even have the best hand. But he'll still lose because he's a lousy coward. He makes me sick.

15. You know she can't do that! Why'd you make her try? She's a woman, can't you see for crying out loud!!?? That closes the case. She'll never be able to do it!

16. The only way Lonnie's going to get a kiss, mistletoe or not, is to sneak up on somebody and throw himself on her so quickly that she can't get out of the way in time.

17. "You're ugly, you're dumb, and you're deformed, Blue. Did somebody have a bad joke in mind when they dreamed you up?"

    "If you are trying to speak euphemistically, Praxton, give it up. That's far beyond your limited capacity. Not sticking your head in the toilet when you go to the john is probably the most complex thought you can handle at one time."

18. Something must have gone wrong. He had on a bullet-proof vest, yet there he is, shot all to pieces. What happened to quality workmanship in American products?

19. You are absolutely beautiful tonight. Gorgeous. You want me to turn the light on now?

20. Your Honor, it is completely obvious that my client is innocent on all counts. Nobody but a mean-spirited jurist could conclude otherwise.

21. It's clear as day to everyone that the governor is hell-bent on destroying the educational integrity of this state! Under his policies, California children will be lucky to be ranked 50th in the nation in terms of academic performance. It makes me wonder whether the man in Sacramento is the real governor or has a switch occurred and the public not been told about it?

22. Hey buddy, want a Hawaiian punch?

23. You are, by far, the best of a sad lot.

24. I've got an old-fashioned fascist for a father. I'm so happy about it that I could cry! I just love it when he restricts me to my room, prohibits all phone calls, and ignores me otherwise.

25. That's it. This pink-elephant team that couldn't beat the girls' tetherball squad has gotten on my nerves! Now if you mild-mannered Clark Kents don't take off those shirts and let your red capes flow to the world, the worst defeat in the history of this school, this universe, will haunt you forever! Are you footballers or are you just fat mounds of flesh and bar-be-que?! Are you going to stand up and be counted? Huh??

CHAPTER FOUR

COMMON DEDUCTIVE FALLACIES

In Informal Logic (logic based on the credibility of the content rather than the correctness of the form) fallacies are mistakes in logical arguments. Those mistakes can damage or destroy an argument's validity or, even if valid, its soundness. Fallacies can make a strong argument weak, and can nullify a weak argument completely. Remember, however, that a fallacy is an argument. There are no fallacious opinions, beliefs, or assertions.

Note: In reality, a fallacious argument can be valid or invalid (but never sound). In this Introductory class, however, to lessen confusion, a fallacious argument will be deemed invalid, and an invalid argument will be fallacious.

The three major categories of fallacies that introductory students should be familiar with are Relevance, Circular Reasoning, and Semantic.

A. FALLACIES OF RELEVANCE

These occur when the premises (evidence) are not very relevant or are not directly connected to the conclusion. Such fallacies are also often called "Missing the Point" mistakes in reasoning. Fallacies of Relevance are most often logical mistakes intended to avoid, or misdirect away from, the real issue. Such fallacies include:

1. The Non Sequitur (It does Not Follow/Irrelevant Reason.) This is the most common fallacious argument and it is the classic model for this category. It is a conclusion based on one thing, idea, or position while the evidence submitted to support that conclusion is tangential at best, and irrelevant (but somewhat related) to the conclusion at worse.

EXAMPLES

a. Mrs. Jones, let me make one thing clear: In this office no one smokes! Got that? And another thing: Because I've had to tell you about this more than once, you go straight to the closet and lock yourself in. And you can't go to the bathroom today either.

b. Come, come, Peter. Don't take it so hard! You knew I had to leave you sooner or later. Taking your car and all the money in your bank account was just so I didn't leave empty-handed. A girl like me has needs, you know.

2. The Ad Hominem fallacy is a response argument aimed at avoiding responsibility or accountability for something. It is most commonly an attack on an opponent's age, character, family, gender, ethnicity, status, dress, appearance, behavior, religion, etc., as a distraction from the real issue at hand.

EXAMPLES

a. Look, fool. You're stupid, ignorant and a fool besides! How dare you ask me about how I spend my money! That's way too complicated for your puny brain. Did you forget to take your medicine this morning, because you are certainly tripping?
b. You don't know me, sir, and nothing you say interests me. You have the nerve to call me a crook, why your whole family is nothing but a witches' coven constantly cooking up bullfrog legs and swamp lies about people. Are you still in the market for a new broomstick?

3. Guilt by Association is a corollary of Ad Hominem. This is a fallacious argument based on an opponent's reputation, the company he/she keeps, etc., rather than the issue at hand.

EXAMPLES

a. He's running for office? Well, hell no, I won't be voting for him! He used to hang around with that group of hooligans on the corner. Nothing good ever came from them, so obviously he can't be worth a quarter.
b. Laura, dear, you can't be a saint in a whorehouse! Your reputation comes from the people you're seen with, so a word to the wise: dump that sucker!!

4. The Genetic fallacy (fallacy of origins) is another corollary of Ad Hominem. It is an argument based on a conclusion about someone's behavior, actions, feelings, intent, etc., because of prior judgments about that person's character rather than focusing on the issue or evidence at hand.

EXAMPLES

a. She couldn't have done that! I know her. She's a nice girl! She sings in the church choir!
b. Here we have a major irony, now don't we? Faculty members who can't write better than freshmen college students and who haven't published anything other than edited books themselves sitting in judgement of people who are real writers trying to make a difference!

5. Tu Quoque (You, too) is a third corollary of Ad Hominem. It is an argument based on avoiding responsibility for something by claiming that others are doing it too.

EXAMPLES

a. Officer, you're not being fair here! Look at all those other people speeding!! Why are you picking on me?

b. Oh, wow, Dr. Horne, what's up? You're not confiscating my paper for cheating are you? I didn't do anything everybody else wasn't doing! As soon as you went out in the hall, they started passing cheat sheets around! You can't blame me for that! I just want an A too!!

6. Ad Baculum (Appeal to Force, Scare Tactics) arguments are ones intended to coerce or force agreement through the use of threat or intimidation, rather than allowing any decision on the merits of the issue at hand.

EXAMPLES

a. Look, that's just the way it is. They want it and you have to comply. Now, if you don't believe me, then go ahead and refuse. See what happens. It'll be your behind for sure, baby. They'll hurt you and I'm not going to be in it.

b. Get down on the ground! Spread 'em! You heard me! Do it or die!

7. Ad Verecundiam (Appeal to Authority) arguments are those which depend upon the usage of prestige, status, respect, or the importance of a proponent or supporter of an argument for that argument's acceptance or rejection.

EXAMPLES

a. My teacher says that I should be proud to be an American, so I guess I will be.

b. The Pope says no sex before marriage for real Christians. Are you ready to marry me, Paul? If not, there will be no business here tonight!

8. Ad Populum (Appeal to Popularity) arguments are those based on the idea that because a majority of people accept a belief, or the position taken in the argument is currently faddish, in vogue or popular, then that is sufficient for the argument's conclusion to be accepted.

EXAMPLES

a. Mom, everybody's down with these Air Jordan sneaks, so you've gotta get me some too! You know I can't go to school wearing stuff from Payless and K-Mart! Are you crazy?

b. Hey, look, Puffy's got some new Sean Johns out and all his rappers are wearing them. That's what I want!!

9. Ad Novarum (Appeal to Newness) arguments are those in which an item's status as new automatically makes it better than other such items (or people, etc.).

EXAMPLES

a. Don't you bring me that junk in here calling it a Christmas present! Swap Meet my foot! If it didn't come straight from Bullocks, I know it isn't squat. Stop being so cheap!

b. Daddy, you can keep your old Mercedes! You look good in it, but not me. I need a new PT Cruiser or at least a Mini Cooper! I can't be looking like some old-school fool!!

10. Ad Misericordiam (Appeal to Pity) arguments are those based on providing emotional excuses connected to extenuating circumstances to justify unacceptable behavior. Not all such appeals are fallacious. They are mistakes in logic when the reasons given bear little relevance to the conclusion.

EXAMPLES

a. Officer, you shouldn't give me a parking ticket! You have a family, don't you? C'mon, you know how it is! I was just gone for a minute or two. I took my crying baby to the candy store to calm him down!!

b. I had to run in and get some milk for this baby before she drove me crazy with her crying. I don't breastfeed, you know. Doctors said it wouldn't be healthy for me or the baby. C'mon. Give me a break!

11. Ad Ignorantiam (Appeal of Ignorance) arguments are those based on accepting lack of evidence against that position as actual or positive evidence against that position.

EXAMPLES

a. Since no one has ever proven that God exists, and I for one have never seen Him, then God must not exist.

b. Since no one has ever proven that God does not exist, and surely rational folk could do that were it true, then it is certain that God does indeed exist!

c. You must be guilty, since you can't prove that you're innocent.

12. Post Hoc Ergo Propter Hoc (After this, therefore because of this) arguments are ones purporting to show causality by mere correlation in time. In other words, because events occurred in a similar time period, one is seen as the cause of the other.

EXAMPLES

a. There was a tremendous bolt of lightning that split Mason's tree yesterday! Right after that his daughter died. Looks like Fate went to punish Mason and hit his daughter instead!

b. I ate a Big Mack, fries and had a supersize drink yesterday, then I got sick as a dog. That food from Mickey Dee's must have been spoiled. It made me sick.

13. Two Wrongs Make a Right is a fallacious argument based on the idea that unacceptable behavior can be and should be excused because it is just a response to a previous act of bad behavior.

EXAMPLES

a. Look, since you hit me with that pillow (and I know you weren't giving me a love tap, here!), I just chopped off your arm. That'll teach you to mess with me!
b. You know you shouldn't have cheated on me. But that's okay. I'm not mad at you. I just slept with all of your friends. We had a chronic party in here last night. I'm sure they'll tell you about it.

B. CIRCULAR REASONING/QUESTIONABLE PREMISES FALLACIES

Circular Reasoning/Questionable Premises Fallacies are those in which an argument assumes its own conclusion (an arguer asserts her conclusion as evidence to prove her conclusion), or in which one accepts the evidence for a position without a solid, rational reason for such acceptance and then uses that to accept a related conclusion. Generally, Circular Reasoning/Q.P. arguments are mistakes in the premises.

1. Begging the Question is the classic example of this type. It is an argument based on merely restating the premises and conclusion as the argument (even though slightly different, but equivalent, words are used).

EXAMPLES

a. In answering the question about why my mouth stayed so dry, my doctor said it was my salivary glands. They were not producing enough saliva. (*Claim:* Your salivary glands must not be producing enough saliva to keep your mouth dry. *Premises:* Your mouth stays dry because your salivary glands are not producing enough saliva. *Question:* Why must your salivary glands not be producing enough saliva to keep your mouth from being dry? Because it just isn't producing enough saliva.)
b. Public nudity is immoral because it is just plain wrong and sinful! (*Claim:* Public nudity must be immoral/wrong. *Premises*: Public nudity is wrong and public nudity is sinful. *Question:* Why must public nudity be immoral and sinful? Because it is immoral and wrong.)
c. I don't believe Anita Hill is lying! Why would she lie? So, it's Judge Thomas who was lying! (*Claim:* Judge Thomas must be lying. *Premises:* I don't believe Anita Hill is lying and she has no reason to lie. It is Judge Thomas who lies. *Question:* Why must Judge Thomas be lying? Because he's a liar and Anita Hill is not.)

2. The Straw Man fallacy is a response argument based on identifying a small part of an opponent's prior argument, then attacking that part in exaggeration as if it is the real issue at hand.

EXAMPLES

a. David is adamantly against special pay to attract minority teachers. He says that the argument to do such a thing advocates reverse racism in order to cure the ill effects of traditional racism. (The logical issue is whether special pay will work to attract more minority teachers. David's approach is to identify the argument for special pay as one based on reverse racism, then he attacks that point as if that was the advocate's entire argument. This is similar to identifying the entire affirmative action pro-argument as an advocacy for quotas, then attacking that as the entire affirmative action argument.)

b. I heard what you said! Don't try to deny it! You said anybody who would buy this old clock is really stupid! Well, who are you to call anybody stupid? If there's anybody stupid around here it certainly isn't me! (The logical issue at hand is whether the old clock is worth buying. It is not, "Who can call who stupid?" That's Straw Man.)

3. False Dilemma/False Dichotomy is an argument based on establishing a limited set of options to choose from (usually 2), when in fact there exist several others, then concluding that absent one of those options, the other is the only choice.

EXAMPLES

a. You are looking at this the wrong way. If you think education is expensive, try ignorance.
b. Listen, this is the way it is. America, love it or leave it!

4. Inconsistency/Double Standard is an argument based on contradictory positions. Sometimes this occurs within the same argument or between two or more arguments by the same person over time.

EXAMPLES

a. "I believe strongly in the right to dissent, however, I do not believe it should be exercised, and when it is, it should be punished appropriately."

b. "I plead guilty, your Honor, with an explanation. I'm innocent. I didn't do it. I couldn't have harmed that child."

5. Slippery Slope is an argument based on concluding a position through connecting a series of hypothetical premises in such a way that if you accept the connected premises you must accept the conclusion. Such arguments are often valid, but are based on false or questionable premises.

EXAMPLES

a. If you step in here, you'll break your foot. Breaking your foot means you'll scream out in pain and therefore disturb daddy sleeping. Then we'll all be in trouble. So don't you dare step in here and get us in trouble!

b. The reason for the defeat: the mighty horse went lame. Without a horse, there was no rider, and because no rider came, there was no message to name. Without a message, there was no one else to blame, so the King lost the war, his country and his claim. Because of one dumb horse, there's no miracle, no fame.

6. Reductio Ad Adsurdum arguments (exaggerated slippery slopes) are those in which a series of hypothetical actions are connected to lead to a ridiculous, humorous, or absurd result in order to persuade someone to a position.

EXAMPLES

a. Abortion is wrong and if we allow it, we'll simply create Sodom and Gomorrah anew, destroying this country in a big sexual bevy of orgies, prostitution, loose morals, and debauchery. America will become one big G-string! End abortion!!

b. Look, I'm not going to beg you. But, it's like this. If you don't sleep with me, I'll take it as another psychological rejection. I've been rejected all my life, and a man can only stand so much. Sooner or later I'm going to rip my clothes off and run buck naked through the streets of this town yelling your name as the one who caused me to finally lose it all. They'll put me on the six o'clock news, nude, crazy, and muttering, Debbie! Debbie! Why did you treat me so bad??!

7. Extension fallacies are those in which a position or point is held to account or attacked/criticized for not doing something which in fact it was never intended to do. In other words, you stretch or extend the boundaries of a position and then attack it once you have stretched it beyond its intended limits.

EXAMPLES

a. Susan just couldn't understand it. They must be prejudiced or something. She had gone to the school and asked for her money after reading the school's colorful brochure that invited members of the community to come and share in the financially rewarding educational experience the school offered. She had assured them that she was a community member and that she was quite willing to share in the school's financial rewards. When she became insistent, they had called security on her and escorted her off campus. She was a bit upset about that.

b. I know you don't like me, and I certainly don't like you. Let's agree to that, shall we? Now then, get on your little motor bike and leave my house immediately. You are not to call my daughter, try and see my daughter, nor ever darken our door again!! That is appropriate.

8. Appeal to Belief is a fallacious argument based on supporting a position principally because it is an accepted, commonly held position (e.g., "Everybody knows this, so it must be true"). This fallacy is one of the consequences of a Proof Surrogate slanter that acquires a little evidence.

EXAMPLES

a. John is a real womanizer, Mary! Everybody knows it but you! Wake up!

b. My money is missing from the safe, Drexler. Only you and I have the combination. Now you and I both know who took it, now don't we?

9. Appeal to the Consequences of Belief is an argument that concludes a position to be the case because not to conclude it would result in negative and adverse circumstances. This fallacy is similar to Ad Ignorantiam: ATCB argues from the negative to get a positive conclusion, and hypothesizes about results that did not occur or have not occurred. It is also the most common way of putting forth an argument about what could have happened if certain situations hadn't occurred, or what can happen if situations and circumstances don't change. Thus, the central problem with this fallacy is that it frequently argues from a position that did not or has not occurred.

EXAMPLES

a. Look, it must be true. Lady Blue is dead. If she weren't dead she would have poisoned us all by now and we are all still alive! (The claim here is, "Lady Blue must be dead." The evidence is that "if she weren't dead, we would all be dead, but we are all alive." The evidence offers a negative presumption to get to a positive result.)

b. If Hitler hadn't ordered the Jews to be exterminated in Germany, the entire history of the Western World would be different! So, Hitler changed the course of history!

10. Taking Out of Context is a response argument based on selecting a partial quote or phrase from a person's prior position and then attacking/criticizing someone's position based on that selection. Also known as "misquoting," it is similar to Straw Man in this regard, but distinctly different otherwise. TOC depends on a written or stated position by someone being isolated from the rest of the information that person presented. This isolated portion is then used to demonstrate an example of how the person being criticized thinks or operates. By contrast, in Straw Man, the selected or isolated portion is attacked or criticized as the prior presenter's entire argument, not just a sample of how he/she thinks or operates.

EXAMPLES

a. "Mr. Jones, now as I remember it, you just said that abortion is murder. Isn't that a position no serious candidate for office should take Mr. Jones? Aren't you committing electoral suicide?" Mr. Jones, in reply, says that the entire point was that abortion is murder to some advocates, himself not included!

b. *Headline:* Senator accuses colleague of advocating child molestation by Catholic priests as an American pastime. *Story:* In her speech yesterday to the assembled Catholic priests of New York, Senator Clinton stated that in the mind of too many Americans viewing the Catholic Church from the outside, the view nowadays was of an institution allowing priests to freely molest our children who come to the Church for sustenance and guidance as if that is the daily pastime of the Catholic clergy. The Church is better than that, and it should stand up for itself.

C. SEMANTIC FALLACIES

Semantic Fallacies are those in which vagueness, multiple meanings, and misleading usage deliberately lead to deception and confusion in reasoning. Semantic fallacies often appear to be and sometimes are valid, but they are not sound.

1. Equivocation, the classic example of this type, is an argument based on a deliberate attempt to manipulate or compel compliance (acceptance) with a position through confusion and ambiguous usage.

EXAMPLES

a. Listen, it makes no sense to quibble over words here, and my calling you a fool is no big deal. It's just a word! Everybody can be fooled at some time or another, including me!

b. No interest payment until 2025!! This is the future of credit payments!—Then, in small print: The interest payment option is entirely dependent on a customer paying 98% of the purchase price in cash before receiving the item.

2. Composition is an argument based on saying that the characteristics of one or more parts of something or someone has the same characteristics as the whole.

EXAMPLE

a. This book must be well written, because every sentence I've seen in it is well written.

b. You gave me nothing but trouble when you were in my class, so I know anybody else from your family will be just as irritating as you were.

3. Division is an argument based on saying that the characteristics of the whole of something or someone are the same for all of its parts.

EXAMPLES

a. Every sentence in this book must be in English, and hard-to-read English at that, since I know for a fact that this is an English book and that means it is written in English!

b. All the latest stats say that young Black men are bound for jail either sooner or later. So, when are you getting locked up, Cleve?

4. False Analogy is a semantic argument based on deceptively comparing one or several of the characteristics of a situation, event, idea, or person with that of another. It is the argument version of the Persuasive Comparison slanter.

EXAMPLES

a. The American colonies fought for their independence in 1776, and just like them the American Football League is now fighting for its freedom and independence. Both were just and honorable causes.

b. You're just like a walrus eating peanut butter—blubbery, icky, and disgusting! Who would want you? Nobody but a truly desperate freak happy to get any attention from anything!

5. False Consolation (Count Your Blessings Fallacy) arguments are those based on misleadingly comparing how much worse one situation or behavior is to the one being criticized, thus discrediting that criticism.

EXAMPLES

a. Look, baby so I don't shave and I watch football and basketball games a lot on weekends. At least you've got somebody decent to be with. Look at your sister and that crackhead roommate she's got. He's always in jail or something!

b. Charlotte! Now have a tantrum if you want to, but there won't be any other ways for you to get to the prom. Your mother is taking you and will pick you up, and that's that! You've got decent transportation there and back and you can go! Everybody can't say that. You should be grateful!

Below is a series of fallacious arguments. From the list provided, please identify the primary fallacy or fallacies committed in each example. Simply place the alphabet of the chosen fallacy next to the item.

    a. Equivocation
    b. Begging the Question
    c. Composition
    d. Division
    e. Tu Quoque (You, too)
    f. Appeal to the Consequences of Belief
    g. Ad Hominem
    h. Guilt by Association
    i. Genetic
    j. Non Sequitur/Irrelevant Reason
    k. Ad Verecundiam (Appeal to Authority)
    l. Ad Baculum (Appeal to Intimidation)
    m. Ad Populum (Appeal to Most People, or Popularity)
    n. Ad Ignorantiam (Appeal to Ignorance)
    o. Ad Misericordiam (Appeal to Pity)
    p. False Analogy
    q. False Dilemma
    r. Post Hoc Ergo Propter Hoc
    s. Slippery Slope
    t. Straw Man
    u. Inconsistency/Double Standard
    v. Two Wrongs Make a Right
    w. Extension
    x. Reductio Ad Absurdum (Appeal to the Absurd or Ridiculous)
    y. Appeal to Belief
    z. Quoted Out of Context
  aa. Ad Novarum
  bb. False Consolation

1. Look, I'm sick of you and your insensitivity. And come to think of it, I'm sick of your ungrateful attitude around here too. And while I'm at it, I'm thoroughly sick of you! I should have known that a man as inconsiderate as you was rotten through and through. You're not just one pain, you're a whole migraine!!

2. Look, Dr. Lyles, I'm sorry I missed your test. But it was like this. I had to save a student's life today, and that's why I couldn't get here. This girl, you know, she needed a ride home, and once I took her, then she needed some money, then she needed me to stay with her until her folks got back home or she said she'd die for sure. You wouldn't want me to leave someone like that without helping her through, now would you? I think I should get some sort of medal, don't you?

3. Feathers are very light in weight, and since children can pick up light things, I'm sure that my two-year old son can lift a whole ton of feathers.

4. "How do you know that God exists?" says One. "Because the Bible tells me he does," says the Other. "Okay, fine. But how do you know that the Bible is true, huh?" says One. "Look, fool! God doesn't lie!" says the Other. "And the Bible is the word of God. That's good enough for me! And it should be good enough for you!"

5. "A good physician certainly cures most of his patients," Bosely argued. "After all, we all know that if he's good, then he has to have a sound medical education, and a man with such a sound background has to be a good physician who can cure most of the patients."

6. I know for a fact that James Brody is a crook and a no-account scoundrel. How do I know? Why look at the company he keeps! Convicts and tax-evaders all! A man is known by his friends, after all.

7. Why, you can't criticize Mr. Nixon for impounding the budgetary funds! Congress wouldn't act! Mr. Nixon is the people's representative. In order to get on with the government, he had to exert his presidential authority and freeze all government expenditures, big and small, just like every other strong president before him has done. He's doing it to force Congress to finish the whole budgetary process and send him a document he can sign. He did it for the good of the country, and the ends justify the means.

8. Harriet: "Hey, what's with all this junk food you just brought? Aren't you the one who's always railing on at me about eating healthy food?"

   Bea: "Aw, don't fuss so. It was just on sale. I got a real bargain on these chips and dip!"
   Harriet: "Oh."

9. Senator Sam Ervin's explanation to a group of women upset over the delay in passing the ERA: "Why, ladies, any bill that lies around here for 47 years or more without getting passed obviously shouldn't be passed at all! Why, I consider that positive proof that the darn thing is unworthy of serious consideration."

10. Lewis Carroll, in *Through the Looking Glass:* "You couldn't jam it even if you wanted to," the Queen said. "The rule is jam tomorrow and jam yesterday—but never jam today!"

    "It must come sometimes to jam today," Alice objected.

    "No, it can't," said the Queen. "It's jam every other day; today isn't every other day, you know."

11. Boy: "Mom, you're always saying you're sick of this sick society, right? . . . And I'm a member of society, right? . . . Well, then I'm sick too and you shouldn't make me go to school where I'll get sicker with those society people!! I don't want to go to school!"

12. Mr. Otis: "We would like to know what the Bible really means to you, Mr. President."

    Mr. Reagan: "Well, I've never had any doubt about it being of divine origin. And to those who do doubt it, I challenge them to show me any similar collection of writings that have lasted for as many thousands of years as the Bible has and still is the best seller worldwide! It had to be of divine origin!"

13. If you think education is expensive, you should try ignorance! The former will toast your jelly. With ignorance, you will pay and pay and pay and pay, ad infinitum.

14. I asked my doctor why my mouth was dry. My doctor said it was because my salivary glands were not producing enough saliva to keep my mouth from being dry. Great doctor, huh?

15. Lyndon Johnson, former president: "I believe in the right to dissent, but I do not believe it should be exercised, and when it is, it should be punished severely."

16. Patient: "Doctor, my wife left me four months ago, and I've been depressed ever since. I'm beginning to wonder. Will I ever pull out of this blue funk?"

    Doctor: "It's normal to feel a lot of anxiety and depression after a severe loss like that. But let me assure you that everyone does recover from this sort of thing. So you will, too. Unless, of course, the trauma has been so severe that your ego is shattered, then of course you have a real problem."

17. "Hunting immoral? Why should I believe that coming from you? You fish, don't you?"

18. "I don't care how serious they appear; anybody who's raking in as much money as those television evangelists can't really care about being ministers for plain, ordinary folks. I don't buy it."

19. Rita: "Four A.M.? Are you serious? Do we really have to start that early in the morning? What's the rush? Wouldn't it make more sense to sleep a little longer and leave a little later?"

    Boyd: "Get off it, Ree! I know you! You want to stay in bed until noon and then drag in at the conference at 12 midnight! Fine, but count me out! Go by yourself! To get there at a reasonable hour, we have to leave real early and not spend the whole day sleeping."

20. We should impeach the Attorney General. Despite the fact that there have been many allegations of unethical conduct on his part, he has not done anything to demonstrate his innocence. That means he's dead sure guilty of wrongdoing!

21. "Are you going to take Dr. Blake for Geography 2 this summer?"

    "Yeah, I heard he's okay."

    "Well, I had him last semester. He is pretty good but, one thing though, he'll spend a lot of time harping on ecology and the environment."

    "Phooey! Those environment guys tell us the water's bad, the air's bad, the world's not fit for dogs. Cheez! If we believe all the malarkey they give us, we'll go crazy worrying about it all! I just can't buy all that ecology crap."

    "Well, maybe. His class is still worth taking, though."

22. Since we are purposeful creatures and we are parts of the universe, the universe must be purposeful as well.

23. There is no definite link between smoking and lung cancer, despite the surgeon general's report and years of scientific studies. Therefore, smoking is not harmful to your lungs. It's okay to buy more cigarettes.

24. Leonardo da Vinci, J.M. Keynes, and Truman Capote were all homosexuals, according to the historical record. They were also great artists and writers. Clearly then, homosexuals are more creative than the general population.

25. Look, young lady, I'm the adult here. I'm grown and this is my house. You won't bring that trash back in here unless you are ready to move out and to get a job! Do you understand me? That boy is no good and I won't have you seeing him! Is that clear?

26. Well, all I know is that eating a piece of pie sure helps my digestion. So, sure, bring me that whole lemon pie over there. If I eat the whole thing I should never have indigestion again!

27. Officer, I was only driving three miles per hour over the speed limit. That's hardly breaking the law, now come on! The car in the next lane was racing much faster than me, yet you pulled me over and not him. He should have gotten this ticket, not me.

28. While the nuclear power plant has been shut down since the last radiation leak, local residents are still getting their electricity from alternative sources. The good weather and pretty scenery in the area, plus ideal shopping and recreation facilities, mean that citizens should not worry excessively about the on-again, off-again status of a single nuclear reactor in the neighborhood.

29. It is a mistake to think that two wrongs don't ever make a right. When we engage in civil disobedience to protest against an unjust law, we break the law as soon as we protest, and thus the protest becomes a second "wrong." Yet surely civil disobedience is justified in such cases. Therefore, in this case, two wrongs do make a right!

30. We cannot allow our school system to become bilingual. If we permit instruction in either of two languages, then what's to prevent the introduction of a third or even a fourth language? Every ethnic group would want its language taught in the schools if we allowed that. Think of the resulting ethnic Tower of Babble we'd have in the schools. I say no. We must keep our schools monolingual. English for everybody!

31. Ms. Wasserberger, you've got to believe me! I meant to turn my essay in on time, but my dog got sick. And I know that's not a big thing to you, but when he's sick, he can't watch my apartment, and so somebody broke in while I was at the library doing research for your essay. Can I turn it in next week? My apartment is such a mess now that I can't get any work done there. You understand, don't you?

32. Logicians claim that the study of argument is an indispensable part of everyone's education. Since this helps to keep those same logicians employed, it is not surprising in the least that they would take this position. Let's not be influenced by such blatantly self-interested views.

33. Limp-wristed, quiche-eating Californians are incapable of serious thought. They're all flakes! To learn anything about politics or the real world, you have to talk to a New Yorker.

34. Marriages are like horses. Some are sure things, while others are losers straight out of the gate. The point is, you should check out the contestants thoroughly before you place your bets.

35. This book is written in English, so I know that I can read it because every sentence in it must be in English too.

36. Every time I eat that cafeteria food, I get seriously sick. No more. I'm going to go to Mickie D's from now on! That cafeteria slop will kill me otherwise!

37. Look, if the idea came from Bob, forget it. Bob hasn't had a coherent thought since he started seeing Gracie. The man is a love slave!

38. More people drive Chevrolets than any other American car. Shouldn't you?

39. My teacher says Jack is a stupid S.O.B. That settles it for me.

40. Rev. Miles is dead set against boozing and fornication. But he's a former pimp. He had 30 girls in his stable at one time. How can anyone believe him? Once a pimp, always a pimp, I say!

41. Look! Get off my back! I'm not abusing you, I'm not stealing your money, and I come home at night. I don't sleep around. So I have a mistress every now and then, and I get a little high. I mean, nobody's perfect, so what's the big deal??

42. Everybody knows that Edgar is a great athlete. It's common knowledge. Based on that, I'm going to give that young man a full scholarship to Compton University.

REFERENCE EXAMPLES

SLANTERS, ARGUMENTS, VALID AND SOUND ARGUMENTS, AND FALLACIOUS ARGUMENTS

TEN S & T'S

1. Jesse is a low-down dirty thief. (P.D./Dysph)
2. Like bad things blown in my face during a Santa Ana, here you are again. (P.C.)
3. You scored the most points ever recorded in history with a hockey stick, but you're still an ugly frog who can't get a girl. (Hyper./P.D./Dysph)
4. Know why you got the boot out of here? Because you lied and got caught, that's why! (P.E.)
5. Obviously, you will not get that job, but maybe, just maybe you'll get another one soon. (P.S./Wease.)
6. Oh, I heard you danced very well last night. The steroids worked, huh? (D Play)
7. The moon was full and Jay was in his element, easing through the bushes in his hairy costume looking for human contact. (Jay was a werewolf. Euphem.)
8. "Oh, hello, Harry," his pretty ex-wife said cheerily, "Come on, I'll introduce you to my new friend, someone who can still get it up regularly." (Innuen.)
9. Hey, you jocks, show some intelligence for once! (Stereo.)
10. You know what, Blue, you could really help your face out a lot if you introduced it to a little soap and water occasionally. (Innuen.)

S & T'S INTO ARGUMENTS

1. Since Jesse just slim-jimmed Kathy's car, ripping out her precious BOSE sound system, and is now running down the street with it, he must be called what he is, a low-down, dirty thief.
2. You should not be here bothering me again! I get bad things blown in my face a lot of times when the Santa Ana winds come, and that's just life. But you, to me you are just a pest!! I should not have to be bothered with something like you!
3. You're great with a hockey stick; why, you scored the most points ever totaled. But you are clearly still a loser. You remain an ugly toad who can't get himself a date, no matter what!
4. People who lie and get caught should get appropriately punished, like getting kicked out. That's what just happened to you.

5. It's clear you won't get that job. There are, of course, other jobs you are qualified for, so I think that perhaps you will be successful elsewhere.

6. You took steroids to help you perform better last night. I heard that you danced very well, indeed. The steroids must have worked, huh?

7. During full moon times, Jay had to go running outside through the bushes in his hairy costume. After all, that's what werewolf people like Jay have to do. Well, he's outside running in the dark again.

8. "Oh, hello, Harry," his pretty ex-wife said. "Come on and let me introduce you to a better man than you ever were. He can still get it up regularly."

9. "Hey, you jocks, show some intelligence for once! You know what they say! Once a dumb jock, always a dumb jock! So, stop proving them right, okay?

10. "Hey, Blue, you need to wash your face sometimes, man. Anyone who wants to look a little better and actually have some friends would take my advice to heart, man."

ARGUMENTS INTO VALID ARGUMENTS

1. People who do what Jesse just did with Kathy's car are nothing but low-down, dirty thieves, period. Why, Jesse just slim-jimmed Kathy's car, ripping out her precious BOSE sound system, and is now running down the street with it. Man, you know he's got to be nothing but a low-down, dirty thief to do that!!

2. You should not be here bothering me again! I get bad things blown in my face a lot of times when the Santa Ana winds come, and I can take that because it's just life. But you, to me you are just a pest !! I should not have to be bothered with something like you! You are not just life, you are a choice, and I choose not to be bothered.

3. You're great with a hockey stick; why, you scored the most points ever totaled. But scoring the most points can't change you from what you really are and will remain: an ugly toad of a loser who can't get a date!! So, listen to me now, you will remain an ugly toad who can't get himself a date, no matter what!

4. People who lie and get caught should get appropriately punished, like getting kicked out. You lied, got caught at it, and got booted out. You got the appropriate punishment you should have received.

5. It's clear you didn't get that job. Move on and forget it. There are, of course, other jobs you are qualified for, so you should be successful elsewhere once you apply to other places and forget this one ever happened. Understand me completely, forgetting this rejection is necessary for your future success.

6. Whenever you take steroids you tend to dance better in your performances. You took steroids to help you perform better last night. I heard that you danced very well, indeed. The steroids must have worked, huh?

7. Whenever the full moon lights the night sky, Jay has to go running outside through the bushes in his hairy costume. After all, that's what werewolf people like Jay have to do. Well, the full moon is lighting the sky this night, so Jay's got to get outside in the bushes and go running in the dark again.

8. "Oh, hello, Harry," his pretty ex-wife said. "Remember when I kept telling you that the man I had to have could get it up and keep it up for as long as I needed it up? And that's the kind of man I knew was better for me? Well, since you couldn't do that, come on and let me introduce you to a better man than you ever were with me. Unlike you, Harry, he can still get it up and keep it up."

9. "Hey, you jocks, show some intelligence for once! Do something smart and pass your midterms!! You know what they say! Once a dumb jock, always a dumb jock! You can prove them wrong if you just stop acting dumb all the time and pass those exams! So, let's stop proving 'em right and instead prove 'em wrong, okay?"

10. "Hey, Blue, you need to wash your face sometimes, man. A lot of people who want to look a little better and actually have some friends would take my advice to heart, man, and you better do it too. Washing your face is what you need to do to look better and have a few friends, fool."

VALID ARGUMENTS INTO SOUND ARGUMENTS

Remember that there are both Sound Arguments (content verified) and Contingently Sound Arguments (content verifiable).

1. According to the LAPD's most recent crime report, people who do what Jesse just did with Kathy's car are nothing but low-down, dirty thieves, period. Why, Jesse just slim-jimmed Kathy's car, ripping out her precious BOSE sound system, and is now running down the street with it. Man, you know he's got to be nothing but a low-down, dirty thief to do that!! And there were at least four eye witnesses who know Jesse, so he can't say, "It wasn't me!" (Sound; Content Verified)

2. You should not be here bothering me again! I get bad things blown in my face a lot of times when the Santa Ana winds come, and I can take that because it's just life. But you, to me you are just a pest! I should not have to be bothered with something like you! You are not just life, you are a choice, and I choose not to be bothered!! (Sound As Is; Content Verified)

3. You're great with a hockey stick; why, you scored the most points ever totaled. But scoring the most points can't change you from what you really are and will remain: an ugly toad of a loser who can't get a date!! Here are ten prior examples of people who looked just like you and who were labeled notorious ugly toads. According to their biographies, they all spent their lives alone and unloved. So will you. So, listen to me now, you will remain an ugly toad, no matter what! (Contingently Sound; Content Verifiable)

4. People who lie and get caught should get appropriately punished, like getting kicked out. That's the cardinal rule of this place. You lied, got caught at it, and got booted out. You got the appropriate punishment you should have received. (Sound; Content Verified)

5. It's clear you didn't get that job. Move on and forget it. There are, of course, other jobs you are qualified for, so you should be successful elsewhere once you apply to other places and forget this one ever happened. Understand me completely, forgetting this rejection is necessary for your future success. (Contingently Sound As Is; Content Verifiable)

6. Whenever you take steroids you tend to dance better in your performances. We have fifty prior examples of this. You took steroids to help you perform better last night. I heard that you danced

very well, indeed. The steroids must have worked, huh? (Sound; Content Verified. *Note:* The p.p.o.v. is not "The steroids must have caused you to dance better!")

7. Whenever the full moon lights the night sky, Jay has to go running outside through the bushes in his hairy costume. He's done this for ten straight years. After all, that's what werewolf people like Jay have to do. Well, the full moon is lighting the sky this night, so Jay has to get outside in the bushes and go running in the dark again. (Sound; Content Verified)

8. "Oh, hello, Harry," his pretty ex-wife said. "Remember when I kept telling you that the man I had to have could get it up and keep it up for as long as I needed it up? And that's the kind of man I knew was better for me? Well, since you couldn't do that, come on and let me introduce you to a better man than you ever were with me. Unlike you, Harry, he can still get it up and keep it up." (Contingently Sound As Is: Content Verifiable)

9. "Hey, you jocks, show some intelligence for once! Do something smart and pass your midterms! You know what they say! Once a dumb jock, always a dumb jock! You can prove them wrong if you just stop acting dumb all the time and pass those exams! So, let's stop proving 'em right and instead prove 'em wrong, okay?" (Cannot Be Sound; Moral Judgement, i.e., Right and Wrong)

10. "Hey, Blue, you need to wash your face sometimes, man. A lot of people who want to look a little better and actually have some friends would take my advice to heart, man, so you better do it too. Washing your face is what you need to do to look better and have a few friends, fool. (Contingently Sound As Is; Content Verifiable. *Note:* Premises did not say, "Everyone or Almost Everyone who wants to look . . ." Neither of those can be verified.)

FALLACIOUS ARGUMENTS

1. Everybody knows that people who do what Jesse just did with Kathy's car are nothing but low-down, dirty thieves, period. Why, Jesse just slim-jimmed Kathy's car, ripping out her precious BOSE sound system, and is now running down the street with it. Man, he's just like the rest of his family! You know he's got to be nothing but a low down, dirty thief to do that!! (Appeal to Belief; Division)

2. You should not be here bothering me again! I get bad things blown in my face a lot of times when the Santa Ana winds come, and I can take that because it's just life. But you, to me you are just a pest!! Look at your friends, all of them are pests to the world! I should not have to be bothered with something like you! You are not just life, you are a choice, and I choose not to be bothered. (Guilt by Association)

3. You're great with a hockey stick; why, you scored the most points ever totaled. But scoring the most points can't get you to score with a girl. To do that, you'd have to change from what you really are and will remain: an ugly toad of a loser who can't get a date!! So, listen to me now, you will remain an ugly toad who can't get himself a date, no matter what! (Equivocation; Genetic)

4. People who lie and get caught should get appropriately punished, like getting kicked out. People who lie and don't get caught deserve no punishment, and that's appropriate. You lied, got caught at it, and got booted out. You got the appropriate punishment you should have received. (Inconsistency/Double Standard)

5. It's clear you didn't get that job. Move on and forget it. There are, of course, other jobs you are qualified for, so you should be successful elsewhere once you apply to other places and forget this one ever happened. The people who didn't hire you are just jerks. Understand me completely, forgetting this rejection is necessary for your future success. (Ad hominem)

6. Whenever you take steroids you tend to dance better in your performances. You took steroids to help you perform better last night. I heard that you danced very well, indeed. The steroids made you dance better, huh? (Non Sequitur/Post Hoc)

7. Whenever the full moon lights the night sky, Jay has to go running outside through the bushes in his hairy costume. After all, that's what werewolf people like Jay have to do. If he didn't do this he would be forced to the alternative: attack, maim, and harm hundreds of innocent people who happen to be out at night. Well, the full moon is lighting the sky this night, so Jay's got to get outside in the bushes and go running in the dark again. (Appeal to the Consequences of Belief)

8. "Oh, hello, Harry," his pretty ex-wife said. "Remember when I kept telling you that the man I had to have could get it up and keep it up for as long as I needed it up? And that's the kind of man I knew was better for me? Well, since you couldn't do that, and appreciate the good thing you had in me, come on and let me introduce you to a better man than you ever were with me. Unlike you, Harry, he can still get it up and keep it up." (False Consolation, Two Wrongs)

9. "Hey, you jocks, show some intelligence for once! Do something smart and pass your midterms!! Act like a Jordan or a Bird or an Irving for a change! You know what people say! Once a dumb jock, always a dumb jock! You can prove them wrong if you just stop acting dumb all the time and pass those exams! So, let's stop proving 'em right and instead prove 'em wrong, okay?" (Ad Populum, False Analogy, Appeal to Belief)

10. "Hey, Blue, you need to wash your face sometimes, man. A lot of people who want to look a little better and actually have some friends wash their faces, man, and you better do it too. Washing your face is what you need to do to look better and have a few friends, fool." (Begging the Question)

CHAPTER FIVE

EVALUATING AND CRITIQUING EXTENDED INFORMAL ARGUMENTS

The primary purpose of argument evaluation and critiquing is to determine the validity and credibility (soundness) of claims made and claims supported, what makes them so, and what weakens or strengthens them.

In this introductory text, the process of evaluation and critiquing will be based on the following interrogatives which will be applied to an extended oral or written argument. Learning to apply these yardsticks with skill and adroitness will help immensely in the development of students' abilities to construct their own arguments.

FORMS FOR ARGUMENT EVALUATION

Answer the following questions for each argument being Critiqued or Evaluated. (*Note:* Make sure to first of all determine—identify—whether you have or do not have an argument. The process below only applies if indeed you have an argument.)

1. What precisely is the argument presented? (Identify the p.p.o.v. or conclusion and the primary and secondary premises supporting the conclusion. Restate the argument as accurately as possible without isolating it. Remember Charity, Fidelity, and Balance.)
2. Is the argument presented a valid one? (Does the evidence presented relevantly support and/or lead to the conclusion?)
3. Is the argument sound and/or credible? (i.e., Is the evidence verified or verifiable? Is the evidence "factual," anecdotal, primary, hearsay, based on references, etc.? Is the source of the evidence reliable?)
4. Does the argument's claim go beyond the evidence offered to support it? (Are any fallacies committed in presenting the argument? If so, what impact do these fallacies have in weakening or diluting the argument?)
5. What counterexamples weaken or destroy the argument? (Counterexamples attack the premises/ evidence used.)

EXAMPLE

"You must be a dog, since all men are dogs."

"Well, I hear what you're saying, but have you known all men, been with all men, or even seen all men? If not, how can you make that claim?"

6. What is the best counterargument to destroy or nullify the original argument? (Counterarguments attack the original claim itself. Re-use the evidence already presented, but in a new way, or present new premises.)

EXAMPLE

Maudlin must be crazy. Only a crazy man would talk to his boss like that and then simply sit down at his work station the rest of the day literally refusing to do any more work.

COUNTERARGUMENT

Maudlin must not be crazy. Only someone cool and calm and not crazy would have the nerve to talk to his boss like that and then directly challenge the boss by just sitting down at his work station for the rest of the day and refusing to do any more work.

COUNTEREXAMPLES

These are attacks on the conclusion of an argument by questioning the accuracy and reliability of the premises. Counterexamples are particularly effective when the premises present absolutisms such as, "All dogs are red," "The scarf of gold never changes color," etc. Presenting one or two examples of blue or brown dogs, and a gold scarf that had changed from one color to another would weaken, and possibly destroy, the original arguments presented.

EXAMPLE

"I know what I'm talking about, you hear? All bips are squirts," he yelled. "All of them. And since my sneaks are obviously bips, too, then what I'm styling here must certainly qualify as a beautiful, beautiful squirt!"

COUNTEREXAMPLE

"Maybe so and maybe not," she interjected. "What I put on this morning was certainly a bip, according to the label on the box it came in and on the purchase receipt. It wasn't, however, a squirt. Johnnie Mae had a couple of pair of bips too, and none of hers were squirts either. Maybe yours is a squirt, I don't know. But what I do know is that being a bip certainly doesn't automatically make something a squirt!"

Counterexamples show evidence intended to contradict the premises of an original argument. The greater the specificity or absolutism of the premises, the more likely that part of the argument is vulnerable to a few examples which raise questions about the reliability and accuracy of the conclusion. In essence, counterexamples challenge the conclusion through diluting or destroying the evidence to support it.

EXAMPLE

"I should die. I just know I should. Have I helped anybody? No. Have I done anything significant or noteworthy? No. Would anybody miss me when I'm gone? In fact, does anybody even know I'm here now? Probably not. Then that settles it."

COUNTEREXAMPLE

"Wait. Hold it! You didn't ask me to butt in, but how old are you . . . 25? 30? Sometime, somewhere, you must have helped somebody. Didn't you ever help a kid from crying? Or help someone with a little school work? Didn't you ever have somebody that you liked a lot and who smiled at you, who held your hand, who maybe became very close to you for a while? I know you must have given a little spare change to somebody in need at least once or twice in your life. And I would miss you if you weren't here. I would. Really. You're here now and you matter to me. So wait. Don't do anything drastic. It can't be that bad!?"

COUNTERARGUMENTS

These are attacks on the original conclusion itself by making an argument which starts from and which contradicts the essence of the original conclusion/p.p.o.v. The aim is to disprove, destroy, or refute that original argument. To make a counterargument, the basic requirement is that you must directly challenge and reverse the original claim/p.p.o.v., otherwise what you have is an alternative argument, not a counterargument. Thus, "The sun must be shining today," has to be countered with, "The sun must not be shining today" or "The sun cannot be shining today," in order to be the claim/conclusion/p.p.o.v. of an appropriate counterargument. Saying, "The sun is not that bright today," or "Today is a cloudy day," or any similar claim, while relevant to the original p.p.o.v., is the beginning of a different and alternative argument rather than a counterargument, and it leaves the original claim unscathed.

Sometimes the same evidence from the original argument is used to argue a different or counter position, but more often the opposing or counterargument brings in new or previously overlooked evidence to make its counterpoint. The crucial idea in a counterargument, however, is that it must start from the conclusion of the original argument.

EXAMPLES

    a. Alice was convinced that Sharon had tricked her. Sharon had told her to show up at 10:30 P.M., exactly, in the park, alone, with nothing but a bathing suit on, if she wanted to see the possible U.F.O. Alice had done everything to the letter. But nothing happened. Nobody came, alien or human. She was left standing in the park, in the dark, bikini-clad and feeling foolish.

COUNTERARGUMENT

Alice was wrong, Sharon had not tricked her. Sharon had told Alice to be there in her bathing suit on Tuesday night at 10:30 P.M., during the last phase of the full moon. Alice, however, figuring any night was as good as another, showed up on Thursday night.

b. Bob was devastated. He had come home early, heard sounds of pleasure coming from his bedroom, and just knew without being told that his one true love had betrayed him again. This was the third time. And this after she had promised him faithfully that she would never hurt him again.

COUNTERARGUMENT

Bob should not have been devastated. His true love did not and could not have betrayed him that day. She was in jail, the victim of mistaken identity in a drug deal gone bad. The police had confiscated her assets, including her car and the keys to the home she shared with Bob. Undercover agents were now using it in a sting operation, and it was they Bob heard in his bedroom, not his one true love.

Counterexamples always aim at weakening an original argument, and counterarguments aim at destroying or nullifying an original argument. However, the end result can be one of three options: both counterexamples and counterarguments can weaken (dilute), wipe out (devastate or destroy), or have virtually no impact on original arguments. To determine the degree of impact, the strength or moderateness of the original argument status and the argument's aim should be identified at the outset and taken into account in conjunction with the damage done to that status and to that aim by the quality, quantity, and credibility of the counter position presented. As is obvious, strong original arguments are usually very difficult to destroy but are relatively easy to weaken. Moderate arguments are easiest to destroy or to bring into serious re-consideration. Properly done counterarguments very frequently do serious damage to arguments which start off weak or moderate.

EXAMPLE: STRONG ARGUMENT WEAKENED

James is heading into serious trouble in his logic course. He hadn't been attending regularly, he hadn't turned in but a few of his assignments, and he didn't show up for today's midterm examination. If previous logic classes are a reference point, James is heading directly for an F in the class.

COUNTERARGUMENT

In fact, James is not heading into serious trouble in his logic course. James isn't like other people; he still has time left in the semester to make up all of the work he has missed thus far, including the midterm. James should not flunk the class. All he has to do is consult with the teacher, get permission to make up all of the past work, catch up with the class readings, and then turn in all of the upcoming assignments.

EXAMPLE 2: STRONG ARGUMENT DESTROYED

Rusty was certain he was the town hero, the best thing to ever happen to Riverdale. He was lauded in both of the town's newspapers and given a long parade through the city last week. He was even interviewed on *60 Minutes,* for goodness sakes, and he came out like a champ. He's got a chest full of medals from 'Nam, including a Purple Heart, and he tells great war stories.

COUNTERARGUMENT

Rusty was not and could not be certain about being the Riverdale town hero. In fact, Rusty was clearly wrong in believing he was the hero, because Rusty was a hero only in his own mind. Rusty didn't go to 'Nam or to any other war. There is no record of him serving in the U.S. Armed Services at any time, according to the U.S. Department of Defense. The news articles were about someone else, not Rusty, and Rusty self-reported the *60 Minutes* interview. Rusty said it was only shown on cable T.V. And, according to the owner of the Surplus Store, Rusty bought all of those pretty medals he had. Did you ever wonder why none of the medals has his name on them? And where are his dogs tags, huh?

EXAMPLE 3: WEAK, MODERATE ARGUMENT DESTROYED

Jay is a better quarterback than Todd is. Why, just a few days ago, Jay threw for 380 yards on 24 out of 35 passes. That's hard to beat. Todd hasn't been playing long enough to post those kind of numbers. He's still a raw talent. Maybe one day he'll come up to Jay's level, but right now, Jay is definitely better.

COUNTERARGUMENT

Jay is not a better quarterback than Todd. Now you're right, Jay did throw over 380 yards the other day. But Todd regularly threw for over 300 yards in most of his college games. So, throwing 380 yards for one game is not that big a deal. And besides, when Jay had 380 yards, his team still lost. When Todd plays, his team wins 95% of the time. When Jay is quarterbacking, his team only wins 50% of the time.

EXAMPLE 4: WEAK/MODERATE ARGUMENT UNSCATHED

If Miss Muffett sits on her tuffet today, she's in for a great surprise. She does indeed sit on her tuffet and BOOM! Wheeeee, there she goes in orbit! Look at the surprise on her face!!

INEFFECTIVE COUNTERARGUMENT

This wasn't the first time outside for Miss Muffett to be sitting on a tuffet. Even though it's real windy for tuffets today, Miss Muffett rather enjoyed the ride. Up, up and away! Miss Muffett loved her windy surprise.

EXAMPLE 5: STRONG ARGUMENT UNSCATHED

Abortion is murder, pure and simple. The 23 chromosome pairs needed for life are discernible at conception and a human heart-beat some 3 to 4 weeks later. Brain-wave activity in the fetus can be measured at 8 weeks. When someone with forethought and intent to destroy that life commits abortion, they deliberately kill a breathing, heart-beating, living human being. That's murder, and it's dead wrong.

INEFFECTIVE COUNTERARGUMENT

Nowhere in the Bible is it recorded that abortion is murder. Nowhere. If the Bible is God's word, and we all know it is, and God didn't speak on such an important issue, how can we claim to be so knowledgeable?

FOLLOWING THE PROCESS: EVALUATING/CRITIQUING ARGUMENTS

First Independent College is engaging in fraudulent activity when it regularly cancels classes that students need to graduate. The activity is fraudulent because both the college catalogue and the fall/spring schedules define these courses as necessary for the students to complete successfully in order to earn the relevant program certificate and/or the college A.A. degree; then when students begin to register in the announced classes, the college cancels those classes, saying that not enough students are enrolling fast enough. "Don't promote what you can't back up," is the principle here that the college continues to violate, even when students have turned in written petitions asking that courses listed and announced be reinstated. They are routinely turned down. What clientele is this college serving anyway? Certainly not its students.

1. What is the argument presented? (Making It Explicit)

   a. First Independent College announces in its catalogue and in its semester class schedules courses that students need to take to graduate, then it routinely cancels those courses once students begin to enroll in them.
   b. Students petition the college to reinstate such cancelled courses which the college has listed and announced, but the college routinely refuses to do so.
   c. Regularly canceling the courses that are announced as available prevents students from completing the courses that are necessary to earn certificates or A.A. degrees.
   d. Therefore, First Independent College is routinely engaging in fraudulent activity by violating the principle: Don't promote what you can't back up.

2. Is the argument valid? Yes. The evidence—particularly the operational definition that fraudulent activity equals unfair class cancellations—makes the conclusion/p.p.o.v. mandatory (a certainty).

3. Is the argument sound and/or credible? Not yet, but it can be once the definition and the activity cited are verified by references. Both the definition and the activity are verifiable, so this argument is Contingently Sound.

4. Does the argument claim go beyond the evidence offered to support it? No, it doesn't. Are any common fallacies committed in the argument? No. Once valid and sound (even Contingently Sound), arguments cannot be fallacious.

5. What counterexamples weaken or destroy the argument? First Independent College allows registration in most of the classes it lists and announces, then it only cancels a few such classes, not all of them, when the student enrollment in them is below 15/class by the time of the close of registration. This is the approved policy and procedure at the college, and it is part of the signed contractual agreement with the faculty union on campus.

6. What counterarguments weaken or destroy the argument? In the semester schedule and the college catalogue the warning is printed to students that courses under-enrolled are subject to cancellation. Because of that, FIC is not routinely engaged in fraudulent activity in canceling classes and is not violating the principle, "Don't promote what you can't back up." Secondly, by canceling under-enrolled classes, FIC actually serves its student clientele well, and routinely offers the classes the following semester. All colleges cancel classes as a part of their regular operation, and at FIC, canceling classes is fiscally sound policy for the college, not fraudulent activity. Such activity helps the college maintain the necessary funding to provide other needed student services, like parking, classroom lighting and heating, etc. Thus, class cancellation should not be taken out of the context of a regular college plan of effective and efficient operation. Through such a plan, the student clientele is very well served indeed. The classes students need to graduate are regularly offered; students merely need to plan their registration activities better to enroll in these classes.

A.

Present counterexamples or counterarguments to each of the following arguments. Identify at the outset whether you are aiming at weakening or destroying the original argument.

1. Richard Nixon, former President, on Watergate: "Some people, quite properly appalled at the abuses that occurred, will say that Watergate demonstrated the bankruptcy of the American political system. I believe precisely the opposite is true. Watergate represented a series of illegal acts and bad judgments by a number of individuals. It was the system that has brought these facts to light and that will bring those guilty to justice."

2. The way home is this way. I'm absolutely certain of it. Look, here's the rock I picked up and threw against that old fence over there. And, see there, there's the old burnt-out store from the riots. And there's the bar-be-que pit. Our house is right around the corner. C'mon!

3. Dusty is an excellent hitter and an overall sound player. He is just the kind of man I want on my team. Any manager would want him. Send him up, Sam. And I mean right now.

4. "Mr Knight, I don't mean to be rude, but I'm not interested in a school that just wants to exploit my son and get to the Final Four. My son can help just about any team and he can go to nearly any school he wants. But the thing is, I have to know wherever he goes, the people there will help him to graduate. Without a degree my son will have a very short future, and frankly, I'm not down with that."

5. All dogs have four paws, a tail and a lively disposition. Well, I've got a cat with four paws, a tail and a lively disposition, so I guess my cat is really a dog.

6. Hang 'em! We've had a trial, sort of, and he don't deserve any more than that in light of what he's done. Noose 'em up, I say. If 'en he ain't the right man for this here crime, that's okay, you kin look at his ugly face and just know he done some dirt somewhere to somebody, so what we's doing is bringing him to justice.

7. Contrary to what many believe, dieting actually upsets the biochemical balance of your body and makes it more difficult to lose weight. Dieting, in physiological terms, can make you fatter, and not just because you "cheat" and go off your diet and overeat. No, the actual process of dieting itself can cause you to gain weight. Your body is a balanced machine which will always try to compensate for abuse and neglect, if it can. Starvation simply makes the body store more food more rapidly—mostly as fat—once you start eating again, as the body compensates for the lack of regular food.

8. I don't care what any of you say, I'm going to smoke if and when I want to. I'm grown and I know what I'm doing. We're going to die, anyway, and most of us will die from something or another. Well, we might as well do what we want while we're still here. That's my philosophy.

9. "C'mon baby, don't give me a hard time! Either you will or you won't! What's it gonna be!? You know I love ya and you know you need to keep me satisfied. Otherwise, there's plenty others willing and ready. So, whad up? Huh?"

10. Children watch too much TV, and they are too highly influenced by it. Take for instance a third-grade class in Connecticut which was recently asked, in a spelling bee, to spell the word "relief." All three students asked spelled "relief," R-O-L-A-I-D-S.

B.

Using the method discussed in this chapter, analyze the following arguments.

1. From the 1954 U.S. Supreme Court case *Brown v. Board of Education*:

"Segregation of white and colored children in public schools has a detrimental effect upon the colored children. The impact is greater when it has the sanction of the law; for the policy of separating the races is usually interpreted as denoting the inferiority of the negro group. A sense of inferiority affects the motivation of a child to learn. Segregation with the sanction of law, therefore, has a tendency to retard the educational and mental development of negro children and to deprive them of some of the benefits they would receive in a racially integrated school system."

2. Excerpt from Adolf Hitler's, *Mein Kampf*:

"Nature does not desire the blending of a higher with a lower race, since, if she did, her whole of higher breeding, over perhaps hundreds of thousands of years, might be ruined with one blow."

"Historical experience offers countless proofs of this. It shows with terrifying clarity that in every mingling of Aryan blood with that of lower peoples the result was the end of the cultured people. North America, whose population consists in by far the largest part of Germanic elements who mixed but little with the lower colored peoples, shows a different humanity and culture from Central and South America, where the predominantly Latin immigrants often mixed with the aborigines on a large scale. By this example, we can clearly and distinctly recognize the effect of racial mixture. The Germanic inhabitant of the American continent, who has remained racially pure and unmixed, rose to be master of the continent; he will remain the master as long as he does not fall a victim to defilement of the blood."

3. Whatever men can do, women can do better. Let's start with God. She has created us all as wonderfully complicated living beings with the capacities to think, to shout, to war, to maim, and to procreate, among other activities. Compared to that, what have men done to earn equal respect? Little else but to grab their scrotums in their hands and charge forward, as if that was what the world needed. Sorry men. It ain't selling in Peoria. And our patience (and that of our Mother) is waning. So do something worthwhile before we abandon you for a higher species!

4. Whatever you say, I must disagree. And whatever you ask, I must decline. You are, without a doubt, the single most influential person in my life. Because of you, I have no family: my wife and children said adios the night after you had that, "Hello, guess who I am?" chat with them. I have no job, since my boss took a distinct dislike for you two seconds after you barged into her office threatening to sue her for sexually harassing me. If I knew you, she told me, then obviously I wasn't fit to work for her. I also have no prospects: everything good that used to be in my corner has split on account of your large shadow. I wonder why I've been so blessed?!!

5. To begin with, you can't play. You can't throw, run, jump, kick, block, or tackle! Hell, you can't even chew tobacco right! Then you're a moron. You'd have to be to come out here asking for a tryout right in the middle of my tongue-lashing the current group of clowns I'm stuck with who

keep masquerading as a real team. And to top it off, you're three tons of fun, son. I could roll your mushy body over this here field to kill some of these weeds and crab grass that need cutting, but that's about all you're good for. The answer is Hell, No! Got that? Now get off my field!

6. If you're White, you're right; If you're Brown, stick around; and if you're Black, Get Back! Or is it pay back? Or half back? Or coming back? Either way, I'm right, I'm here and ain't no backtrack.

C.

Below are two controversial, extended arguments. Find at least 15 fallacies and/or slanters (even if the same fallacy or slanter is repeated one or more times). Analyze each argument based on the method presented in the chapter. Compose counterexamples or counterarguments to weaken or refute each argument.

ARGUMENT A

If God had intended for women to be equal, then He'd have made them so. But quite obviously, he didn't do that. In fact, there's no evidence that He ever intended for women to do anything else except to be good makers: home makers and baby makers. That's the only thing that makes sense here. Men as the warriors and breadwinners, and women, their partners, as the rightful keepers of the homestead.

The only real justification we need for this conclusion is the Bible. After all, the Bible is God's word and He passed it on to His true descendants. Its says forthrightly in John III, verses 11 through 15, and I quote, "And he gave his only begotten son, that he should teach the world how to honor God, the Father." Now nowhere in there does it say women are equal, now does it? God, His Son, the Father: All masculine, right? All about men! The only place where women can get in is the begotten part. That's their function. They are the begottees. We, the males, are the begotters. Together, we, through God, the Father, brought Jesus into this world, just as surely as the begotters and the begottees get together and being fine, bright, and wholesome babies into this world. And who cares for the infants? Who guides them through danger and darkness so they can grow up to do God's work? Why, women, that's who! The mothers of us all. That's their real work. Their divine assignment. Their magnificent purpose for which they are on this planet!

Their purpose is not to worry men with this equality foolishness, since history, tradition, and common sense all show that women aren't and won't ever be equal to men. That's against nature and against God's grand design. Why, they shouldn't even waste their time on foolishness like that! Their bodies, their spirits, their very minds are not meant for such blasphemy!

The real issue is how a woman can best carry out her two main functions in life. All else should be and needs to be best left to her companion, her protector, her partner, her man. God's chosen ally on this earth. Amen.

ARGUMENT B

Africa to the East, and Mexico to the West, are the real origin points of AIDS in the world. They both can be considered AIDS central. With their joint contribution, it is the beginning of the end of mankind as we know it. In fact, with so many Africans and Mexicans catching AIDS, then migrating to South America, Europe, America, and the rest of the world, they will infect everybody else in a broad scale Montezuma's voodoo revenge! I say, let's round them all up and kill them before that happens. We can't afford to wait. All true Americans should get themselves a gun and shoot them a wetback, Beaner, Muchacholo, African, Nigra, Spook, Ubangi Lip, or whatever they are calling themselves today.

I know what I'm talking about. Why, Revelations has already forecast the Last Days and that's just where we are right now. And the time to show our real Christian blood is upon us. Strike quick the blow of freedom!! God doesn't like ugly, and we all know who's ugly on this planet, now don't we?

The first time I heard about AIDS in these two places, I knew trouble was headed our way. Those lazy greasers and kinky heads have never been able to keep their zippers up and their dresses down. Now they want us to feel sorry for them. Give them medical aid and treatment.

I say no! The answer is a general "cull and kill." That's how we handle disease in our cattle and sheep, right? Well, if it is good enough for farmers and ranchers of this great country, then by Heaven, it's good enough for me! Wake up, America! Don't be bamboozled by all this talk of ethnic awareness and civil rights! It is our civil right to protect ourselves against this advancing Brown-Black menace! It's the outright moral thing to do. Everybody knows that when a prized pedigree is damaged beyond repair, as much as you may love 'em, you've got to have them put down. They should be put out of their misery before they suffer tremendously, and before they pass on what illness they're got to you. That's what I'm saying here. It's the humanitarian thing to do. Get them before they get you! It'll be a better world, believe me!

D.

Construct a solid argument of 3–5 pages on a contemporary topic of your choosing. Analyze your own argument (or exchange with your classmates and analyze each others').

CHAPTER SIX

FORMAL LOGIC

INTRODUCTION

Formal logic is the study of argument forms, or distinctive patterns of reasoning, based on rules and argument format rather than the semantic content of arguments. For formal arguments to be valid, their presentation must fit the established form or pattern, including adhering to all of the rules associated with that particular pattern.

A primary purpose for studying argument forms is to learn how to organize data consistently into coherent and predictable units of validity. Both formal logic and informal logic use the same basic definitions of arguments—claim and evidence— and most of the rules learned in Part One will also be useful in the study of Formal Logic. However, there is at least one fundamental difference between the two. For the purpose of our introductory discussion here, that principal difference is one of emphasis.

Formal Logic emphasizes whether the content of the argument fits a prescribed logical form or not (i.e., whether the argument as presented fits the package). The actual content of the argument, while not irrelevant, is clearly secondary to the form of the argument.

Informal Logic, on the other hand, is primarily concerned with whether the meaning of the presented content (implied or overt) is logically valid or invalid. Within the different types of informal arguments (e.g., persuasive, explanatory, inferential, discovery, etc.), correct argumentation is a matter of the strength of the relationship between the evidence and the conclusion. Whether the argument is strong, weak, fallacious, valid and/or sound depends solely on that content relationship.

EXAMPLE (INFORMAL)

Harry must have gone home for the day. His attaché case is gone, his keys are not on the desk anymore and the light is out in his office.

While this is obviously an argument on the face of it ("Harry must have gone home," is the p.p.o.v.) it is neither valid nor sound, and the proper evaluation of it requires an assessment of what is coherently missing. In other words, what is the established relationship between the claim and the premises? Ascertaining that there is a missing premise such as, "Whenever Harry's attaché case and keys are gone and his office light is out, then he's gone home," is important in evaluating this argument. You should remember the process for doing this from Part I. There is then a strong relationship between the content evidence and the conclusion, and (within such an inferential premise) we have a valid informal argument which may also be sound (Contingently Sound—depending on the verification of whether he's actually gone home).

A formal argument using the same information would look like this (in this case, a Modus Ponens conditional argument): "If Harry's attaché case and keys are gone, and his office light is out, then Harry's gone home for the day. His case and keys are gone and his office light's out, so I guess he's gone home then." To be valid, this argument depends solely on whether the content presented in the premises and the conclusion fits the Modus Ponens form, and not on the content relevancy associated with whether Harry actually went home.

Reducing the argument's information to "If A, then B. It's A, therefore it must be B," may make it clearer, where A is Harry's attaché case and keys being gone and his office light being out, and B is Harry's having gone home.

The vocabulary to do informal argumentation includes premises, premise indicators, conclusions, conclusion indicators, soundness, and fallacies. The vocabulary to do formal argumentation maintains the former ingredients and adds sentential operators, tildas, sentence letters, conditionals, disjunctives, symbolic/formal sentences and the like. Grasping the vocabulary and syntax (grammar) of formal logic, as you were required to do with valid informal logic, is necessary to use, critique, and evaluate valid argumentation in this arena.

BASIC SYMBOLS IN FORMAL LOGICAL REASONING AND ANALYSIS

NAME OF SYMBOL	EXAMPLE OF SYMBOL	MEANING
Negation Sign (Tilda)	~ or ⌐	It is not the case that . . .
Conjunction (Ampersand)	& or ∧	and
Disjunction (Wedge)	v	Either . . . or
Conditional (horseshoe or arrow)	Þ or →	If . . . then
Parenthesis	( )	Whatever is inside is tied together
Biconditional	≡ or ↔	If and only if

Also important is "unless," which forces a translation of a conditional such that "If apples and oranges, okay, unless pears and prunes; then apples and oranges." The "unless" becomes "If not "and the antecedent, while the part of the statement which precedes the "unless" becomes the consequent.

"Only if" statements also force a specific sentence translation.

EXAMPLE

Only if I go home will I receive my just reward. *Translation:* If I receive my just reward, then I go (or will have gone) home. In statements like these, the phrase which follows the "only if" becomes the consequent, while the phrase which precedes the "only if" becomes the antecedent.

EXAMPLES OF USE

It isn't apples or oranges = ~A v O

It is both apples and oranges = A & O

It is either apples and oranges or pears and prunes = (A & O) v (P & Pr)

If apples, then oranges = A Þ O or A→O

If apples only if oranges = A↔O (which means A→O and O→A)

The symbols shown on the previous page are called sentential operators. The first one, the Tilda, negates the item or sentence in front of which it is placed. It is a unary operator. In other words, it is a single prefix which connects to logical sentences. The other five basic sentential operators shown are binary connectives. They link two or more logical sentences together into compound sentences.

In Formal Logic, a sentence letter such as "p" or "q" represents data. Thus, "If Harry's attaché case and keys are gone and his office light is out, then he's gone home," can be represented as H→G, where H represents everything from "Harry's" to "out," and G, everything from "he's" to "home." The H is a logical sentence phrase, the G is a sentence phrase, and the → is the binary sentential operator which connects them into a compound sentence.

A compound consisting of two logical sentences joined by "and" (the ampersand) is called a conjunction, and its two component sentences are called conjuncts. Conjunction can also be expressed in regular English by "but," "yet," "although," "nevertheless," "whereas," and "moreover." They, like "and," affirm both the statements they join, although they also differ in adding subtle attitudes and emotional content to the words they connect, while "and" stays neutral.

A compound consisting of two statements joined by "either . . . or" is called a disjunction. The form connected with it is called a Disjunctive Syllogism (DS) or, more frequently, and more accurately, a Disjunctive Argument (DA), and the two statements connected are called disjuncts. In the argument, "People are either fat or skinny (but not both), and Polly Person here is certainly not skinny," the conclusion has to be (assuming Polly Person is within the class of people) that Polly Person is therefore fat. The primary thing to remember about disjunctives, particularly exclusive disjuncts, is that the argument identifies either "this" or "that." If it is not "this," then it has to be "that;" and if not "that," then it has to be "this;" no matter how simple or complicated the disjuncts appear to be. However, non-exclusive disjuncts must indicate that it is not one item, and not both, in order to conclude that it must be the remaining disjunct. See note below for further explanation.

Note: There are essentially two basic types of DAs: exclusive and non-exclusive. It is critical, once it is determined that you are dealing with a DA, to simultaneously determine which type of DA it is. Exclusive DAs mean if not one disjunct, then it must be the other. Conversely, if it is one disjunct, then it can't also be the other. Non-exclusive DAs mean that asserting one disjunct does not automatically negate the other. It could be both disjuncts. The principle rule of DAs applies to the non-exclusive, while the exclusive type is most frequently seen as the exception to the rule. The principle is: For a valid DA (Standard DA), one must negate the existence of one disjunct in order to conclude the other.

EXAMPLE 1 (VALID STANDARD DA)

~P [(R v Q) (ZWT→XY) ↔ D] v~ C + B + 10   1000 v 25

~ ~C + B + 10   *or*   ~25

∴ ~ P [(R v Q) (ZWT→XY) ↔ D]   ∴ 1000

EXAMPLE 2 (VALID EXCLUSIVE DA)

A v B (but not both, or bnb)   A v B

 B   *or*   ~A

~A   B

Compound statements linked by "If . . . then" are called conditionals (and are symbolized by the horseshoe or right-pointing arrow). The sentence phrase that follows the "If" is called the antecedent, and the sentence phrase which follows the "Then" (even when the "then" is omitted) is called the consequent. The "If and Then" may be at the beginning, middle, or end of a compound sentence.

EXAMPLES

"If I go, then she will come." "She'll come, if I go." "I wouldn't do that, if I were you." "Were I to jump straight in, then she would swim away."

The Tilda (~) means "it is not the case that" or, abbreviated, it means "not." Thus, Harry negated by ~Harry means it is not the case that Harry, or it's not Harry. The grammatical variations of this include non, no, un-, ir-, in-, im-, and a- used as prefixes to words, although besides negation they may mean other things too. In essence, for Formal Logic true negation means the exact reverse of the logical sentence prefixed. There is no middle ground.

The parentheses are used like commas and other such punctuation in regular English sentences. They are punctuation to avoid ambiguity and confusion in the symbolic sentences.

Finally, the biconditional (if and only if) is used to indicate reciprocity between the antecedent and consequent.

EXAMPLE

1≡2 or 1↔2 means 1→2 and 2→1

These then are the basic vocabulary terms which students must learn in order to grasp and utilize Formal Logic. To be sure, there are other terms to be added along the way, but these are the basics.

Now, let's put them to use.

INTRODUCTION TO SENTENTIAL LOGIC:
ELEMENTARY VALID AND INVALID ARGUMENT PATTERNS

There are three general ground rules for formal logic:

1. All formal logical arguments must have a minimum of 2 premises.
2. The first premise will generally identify the category of the formal logical argument (establishes the relationship between terms and the sentential operators present).
3. The second premise will identify the particular type of argument in that category and the rules to be applied for validity. Although there are many types of formal logical arguments, the five basic groupings of formal logic include:

   1. Conditionals (including Biconditionals, discussed in Chapter 7)
   2. Disjunctives
   3. Conjunctives (See Chapter 7)
   4. Dilemmas
   5. Categoricals

Except for the biconditional, there are three principal conditional patterns: Modus Ponens, Modus Tollens and Chain Arguments (sometimes called Hypothetical Syllogisms). All three share the antecedent and consequent ingredients, all three need at least two premises and a conclusion to be conditional arguments, and all three adhere to the same process rules.

1. The first step in determining the validity/invalidity of formal arguments is to identify the particular kind of argument one has (and whether, in fact, it is an argument). Thus, "If Allen has cats, I expect Mollie to have paws, but Allen doesn't have any cats, so Mollie must be out too." This is a conditional argument since you have the classic "if . . . then" construction with no other intervening types. There is a conclusion and direct evidence bearing on that conclusion (whether or not it "makes sense" in everyday terms). Once you have made this initial determination, move on.
2. Identify the terms in the argument as A, B, C, P, Q, R, etc. Identify the same term used in either one of the premises and/or the conclusion with the same letter. Thus, in the present example, "Allen has cats" can be A and Mollie's paws can be B. So, A→B, ~A, therefore ~B, represents the argument presented (and this is actually an invalid one).
3. Use the information in the second premise (which will say something positive or negative about one of the terms discussed in the first premise, or it will introduce a third term) to determine what particular logical pattern is being used. (Step #1 limits the field while Step #3 gets down to specifics within the selected field. For example, #1 allows a choice between conditionals, conjunctives, disjunctives, syllogisms, etc., while #3 decides what kind of conditional, what kind of disjunctive, and the like. This second premise information should not, at this point, be used to evaluate what is done with the term(s) mentioned, but only used to ascertain that a particular term(s) has in fact been repeated from the first premise.

4. Once the first three steps are completed, the student knows what pattern is present, and can now apply the distinct rules of that pattern to the argument presented. For example, in the A→B, ~A, therefore ~B argument, the second premise (~A) shows that this is a Modus Ponens conditional argument (see explanation below) because the second premise provides evidence about the antecedent. The rules for Modus Ponens arguments state that everything (antecedent and consequent) must be affirmed. The antecedent here is denied, violating the rules, which automatically invalidates a Modus Ponens argument.

5. In dealing with formal arguments, it is useful to start off learning how to evaluate them in stages: stage one is at the premises level, stage two is at the conclusion level. Formal arguments can be valid at stage one, then invalid at stage two, making them invalid overall; and they can be invalid at stage one, thus making further analysis unnecessary.

EXAMPLE

A→B. ~A, therefore ~B is invalid at stage one, the premises level, thus there is no need to evaluate whether the denial of the consequent in the conclusion is valid or not. Had the argument been presented A→B, A, therefore ~B, the first stage evaluation would be valid since the antecedent would have been affirmed as required by the Modus Ponens rules. However, at stage two, or the conclusion, that Modus Ponens argument would be invalid since the consequent is denied, which would still violate the Modus Ponens pattern. Thus, the argument overall would be an invalid M.P. argument.

Follow these rules sequentially. Do not try to shortcut until there has been substantial practice in following the process and correctly evaluating elementary argument patterns. This will allow avoidance of trouble later. It should be noted that the five process steps, while initially discussed specifically for conditionals, should be used with all of the elementary patterns until the student is highly familiar with them.

The other patterns discussed below are Disjunctive Arguments (either . . . or, using the vel sign), Constructive and Destructive Dilemmas (conditionals plus disjunctives), Categorical Claims and Categorical Syllogisms. (As mentioned above, biconditionals and conjunctives are discussed in Chapter 7.) Together they introduce the student to the basic syntax and semantics of Formal (symbolic) Logic.

PATTERN I. MODUS PONENS (MP)

Modus Ponens is generally called the positive conditional. Its pattern is:

R→S		R→S
R	*or*	R
.:. S		S

Both of these, equivalent as they are, are read "If R, then S. It is R, therefore it is S." In order to validate an MP argument, one follows the steps noted above. If the second premise provides data which affirms or agrees with the antecedent (AA), then the MP argument is valid at stage one, the premises level. It then must follow through and affirm the consequent at the conclusion level (AC). The MP is then valid. Thus a valid MP = AA + AC.

It is called the positive conditional because of this characteristic: to be valid each stage is affirm, affirm.

FALLACY OF DENYING THE ANTECEDENT

The MP's primary characteristic is the affirmation of the antecedent. The most common mistake in dealing with MP argument is to deny the antecedent, thus rendering an MP argument invalid at stage one. Even if one affirms the antecedent properly but then denies the consequent at stage two in the conclusion, the argument is still rendered invalid at that level. Mixing positive and negative (affirm and deny) in MP arguments regarding the antecedent and the consequent also invalidates that argument.

PATTERN II. MODUS TOLLENS (MT)

Modus Tollens is often called the negative or reverse conditional. Its pattern is:

$R \rightarrow S$ $R \rightarrow S$

$\sim S$ *or* $\underline{\sim S\ }$

$\therefore \sim R$ $\sim R$

Both of these are read, "If R, then S. It is not S. Therefore, it is not R." For an MT to be valid, again follow the steps noted above. If the second premise provides data that denies or reverses the consequent (DC), then the MT argument is valid at stage one, the premises level. It then must follow through and deny the antecedent at the conclusion level (DA). The MT is then valid. Thus a valid MT = DC + DA. It is called the negative and reverse conditional because of this characteristic: to be valid each stage is deny, deny.

FALLACY OF AFFIRMING THE CONSEQUENT

The most common method of invalidating an MT argument is to AC or affirm the consequent rather than to deny it. This kills the MT argument at the level of the premises and makes further analysis unnecessary.

Additionally, even when the consequent is denied and thus first stage valid, if the antecedent in an MT argument is then affirmed in the conclusion, the argument is still invalid at the second stage. Any mixing of positive and negative (affirm and deny) in an MT argument's relationship to its antecedent and consequent will render the argument invalid. If one AC's instead of DC's, or AA's instead of DA's, the MT is invalid.

PATTERN III: CHAIN ARGUMENT (CA)
(ALSO CALLED HYPOTHETICAL SYLLOGISM OR HS)

The Chain Argument is a series of three or more conditionals such that one can derive the final conditional from combining the original or first antecedent and the last consequent of the others. The CA pattern is:

R→S   R→S

S→T   *or*   S→T

∴ R→T   R→T

Whether there are only three premises or a jillion premises, to have a valid CA, the first consequent must also be the second antecedent, and that pattern must continue throughout the argument. Finally, the antecedent and consequent combined in the conclusion must retain the positions they held in the premises (i.e., the first antecedent must be connected with the last consequent, in that order). This means that the conclusion cannot convert what was an antecedent into a consequent.

EXAMPLE

Correct   Incorrect

B→E   B→E

E→G   E→G

G→H   G→H

H→K   H→K

∴ B→K   K→B

PATTERN IV: DISJUNCTIVE ARGUMENT (DA)
(ALSO KNOWN AS A DISJUNCTIVE SYLLOGISM)

The Disjunctive Argument identifies two alternatives, either this or that. If it is not this, then it has to be that, or if not that, then it has to be this. This rule of the DA pattern pertains no matter the complexity of the alternatives. The pattern is:

B v D   (PvP&J) v~L (T&W + 1)

~D   *or*   ~(PvP&J)

∴ B   ~L (T & W + 1)

This is the Standard DA model. In it, the second premise must always be negated for the Standard DA to be valid. In the other DA, the Exclusive DA (either . . . or, but not both), the valid pattern is:

A v B (bnb)		A v B (bnb)
B	*or*	~A
∴ ~A		B

PATTERN V: CONSTRUCTIVE DILEMMA (CD)

This pattern, though not as commonly used as the previous four, is still important enough to learn. When there are two non-related antecedents, a merging of them as alternatives (disjuncts) causes a corresponding merger of their consequences as alternatives. The pattern is:

Q→H	Apples→Nuts
R→P	Pears→Prunes
Q v R	It will be either Apples v Pears
∴ H v P	It will also be Nuts v Prunes

Combining the first antecedent (Apples) with the second consequent (Prunes), or the first consequent (Nuts) with the second antecedent (Pears) invalidates the Constructive Dilemma.

PATTERN VI: THE DESTRUCTIVE DILEMMA (DD)

The basic pattern of the Destructive Dilemma argument follows that of the Constructive Dilemma, i.e., both antecedents are combined into a disjunct, as are both consequents. The distinctiveness of the DD is the use of the tilda (~) in either the conditional part of the argument, the disjunctive part, or both. For the DD to be valid, besides complying with the regular rules of the Dilemma format—antecedent to antecedent, consequent to consequent—the tildas used must be consistent. Thus, a tildaed antecedent A, must also be tildaed when it is put into a disjunctive.

EXAMPLES

~A→B	~A→ ~B
C→ ~D	~C→D
∴ ~A v C	~ A v ~C
B v ~D	~B v D

For each of the following groups of symbolized claims, identify which of the rules previously presented was used to derive the last line. Was the relevant rule complied with or not?

1. $P \rightarrow (Q \& R)$

   $(Q \& R) \rightarrow (S \lor T)$

   .:. $P \rightarrow (S \lor T)$

2. $(P \& S) \lor (T \rightarrow R)$

   $\sim(P \& S)$

   .:. $(T \rightarrow R)$

3. $P \lor (Q \& R)$

   $(Q \& R) \rightarrow S$

   $P \rightarrow T$

   .:. $S \lor T$

4. $(P \lor R) \rightarrow Q$

   $\sim Q$

   .:. $\sim(P \lor R)$

5. $(Q \rightarrow T) \rightarrow S$

   $R \rightarrow P$

   $\sim S \lor \sim P$

   .:. $\sim(Q \rightarrow T) \lor \sim R$

6. $\sim(Z \& T) \rightarrow \sim(R \& L) + ABC$

   $\underline{\sim \sim(R \& L) + ABC}$

   $\sim (Z \& T)$

7. $(14 + 11 + 30) \rightarrow \sim[(90 + 99) \lor (20 + 58)]$ (bnb)

   $\underline{\sim[(90 + 99) \lor (20 + 58)]}$

   $\sim(14 + 11 + 30)$

8. ABCDE v PRST

   ~PRST

   ABCDE

9. ~ ~Purple & Blue v ~ ~Red & Yellow

   Red & Yellow

   ~Purple & Blue

10. a. Figs→Fat   c. Cat→Hat

    b. Fat→Cat   d. Hat→Mat

    Figs→Mat

Consider these argument forms: Determine whether each is valid/invalid.

a. 1. If 1, then not 2

   2. 1_____

   3. So, not 2

b. 1. If not 1, then 2

   2. 1_____

   3. So, not 2

c. 1. If 1, then not 2

   2. 2_____

   3. So, not 1

d. 1. If not 1, then not 2

   2. Not 1_____

   3. So, 2

e. 1. If 1, then 2

   2. Not 1_____

   3. So, not 2

f. 1. If 1, then 2

   2. 2_____

   3. So, 1

g. 1. If 3, then 25

   2. 20_____

   3. So, ~3

h. 1. (99½ – 10) v .9999

   2. .9999_____

   3. So, ~(99½ – 10)
      (Non-Exclusive)

   i. 1. If not 1, then not 3

       2. <u>Not 1</u>

       3. So, 2

   j. 1. 1, if 2

       2. <u>2</u>

       3. So, 1

   k. 1. If Pink, then Blue Rot

       2. <u>It is Blue Rot</u>

       3. So, it is Pink

   l. 1. PQR v TLM (bnb)

       2. <u>PQR</u>

       3. TLM

  m. 1. Hurricane Lou, only if Me and You

       2. <u>Hurricane Lou</u>

       3. So, it will be Me and You

   n. 1. A$\rightarrow$12345

       2. 12345$\rightarrow$678910

       3. 678910$\rightarrow$No

       4. .∴. No$\rightarrow$A

Translate each of the following sentences into symbolic notation using the suggested symbols as abbreviations, or make up your own.

1. The Reds will win only if the Dodgers collapse. (R, D)
2. The Steelers will win if their defense holds up. (S, D)
3. If it rains or snows, the game will be called off. (R, S, O)
4. Unless there is a panic, stock prices will continue to rise. (P, R)
5. If the house comes up for sale and if I have money in hand, I will bid on it. (S. M. B)
6. You can be a success if you only try. (S, T)
7. You will get a good bargain provided you get there early. (B, E)
8. You cannot lead a happy life without friends. (Let H = You can lead a happy life, and let F = You have friends.)
9. Between me, you and the zoo or him, her and Mr. Sir.
10. Let me be loved or let me be alone unless you promise more.
11. If Ted, then Alice or else Pete, if not Dallas.
12. If one, then the other; if two, then another; so one or two and the other or another. Got that?
13. Either it's not 10 or Patty and 50 or Leon, if it's Zoe, then Frank and Susan, if Tank.
14. This (A + 60 − 90 + P) or That (30 − 20 − 10)
15. If a fool, then a fallow, and if a fallow, then foul fellow, and then fewer I suppose, if foul fellow, so only if fewer, a fool.

CATEGORICAL CLAIMS

A categorical claim says something about groups or classes of things. There are four basic sentence forms which represent the four standard categorical patterns.

A-statements: All _____ are _____.
    Example: All apples are fruit (All S are P)

E-statements: No _____are_____.
    Example: No vegetables are fruit (No S are P)

I-statements: Some _____ are _____.
    Example: Some fruit are apples (Some S are P)

O-statements: Some _____ are not_____.
    Example: Some vegetables are not apples.

The subject term goes into the first blank (e.g., All apples, No vegetables, Some fruit), and the predicate term goes into the second blank, (e.g., are fruit, are apples, are not apples). Only nouns and noun phrases (and occasionally specific pronouns) will work as categorical claims. An adjective, even a predicate adjective, won't do.

Each of the standard four categoricals has its own graphic illustration in a Venn diagram. In the figures below, this is demonstrated. The circles represent the classes or categories named by the term. The shaded areas represent areas that are empty (i.e., not shared between the circles), while the Xs represent areas that contain at least one categorically claimed item. An area that is blank, when contrasted with a shaded portion, is an area that represents what is left after the shaded portion is eliminated from the claim, and when associated with an X, the blank area represents what is not claimed (though the area is not empty). In the diagrams below, students should note that with absolutist claims (A, E) shaded areas are more frequently used, and with the partial claims (I and O) Xs are most commonly used.

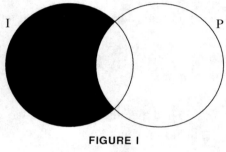

FIGURE I

A-claim: All I are P

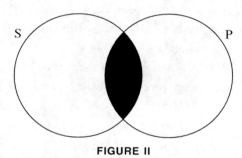

FIGURE II

E-claim: No S are P

Make sure to see that in the A-claim diagram, the area that would contain any members of the S class that were not members of the P class is shaded—that is, it is empty (All that is I is in the category of P. There is no I left that is not part of P). In the same vein, the E-claim diagram, where S and P overlap is empty since any S that would have been a P has been eliminated. (No S are in the category of P).

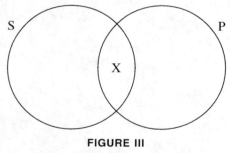

FIGURE III

I-claim: Some S are P

(Some S are in the category of P)

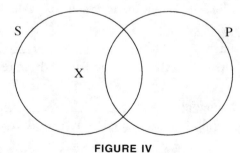

FIGURE IV

O-claim: Some S are not P

(Some S are not in the category of P)

The word "some" means "at least one" within a category. Figure III represents that at least one S is in the category of P, and X marks the interaction and overlap. Figure IV shows that at least one S is outside of the category of P. The other interaction between S and P is not claimed.

The two claims that include parts of classes within another (A and I claims) are affirmative categorical claims, while the two that exclude parts of classes from another (E and O claims) are negative categorical claims.

In everyday language, most of what we say about groups, things, people, or classes of items can be translated into one of these four traditional patterns and can thus be evaluated based on that form. The four basic patterns are very versatile.

There are several helpful hints which should be remembered in translating everyday speech to one of the four traditional statements:

a. All claims like "Only A's are B's" should be translated into an A statement with the term immediately qualified by the "only" becoming the predicate term and the other term becoming the subject.

Example: Only good students will pass this class.
Conversion: All students who pass this class are good students.

b. All claims like "The only A's are B's" should be translated as A statements (All A's are B's) with the term immediately qualified by "the only" becoming the subject term, and the other term becoming the predicate.

Example: The only people who can vote are citizens.
Conversion: All people who vote are citizens.

c. Claims like "Everybody is a winner" is translated into "All bodies are winners."

d. Whenever and wherever statements ("Harry is always a pest whenever he shows up," and "Wherever I see him I get excited" should be translated into A statements. ("All times that Harry shows up are times he is a pest" and "All places that I see him are places that I get excited.")

e. Claims about single individuals or things (meaning exactly one person or thing is in that class of people or things) should be translated as either A or E claims.

Example: "Harry is never on time." (E)
"Harry is the best one!" (A)

f. "Most," "almost," "all," "a lot," "and the like," are clues for I or O statements.

Example: "Most of you will be fired" becomes "Some of you are those who will be fired."

Translate the following items into a standard-form claim. Do not violate any of the rules previously provided for translating/using the four basic forms.

1. The murder suspect is not Sally's uncle.
2. Nobody came to the party but friends of Fred.
3. Whenever there are people and water, there will be mosquitoes.
4. Most of you will not understand these terms.
5. Oxygen is essential to human life.
6. Except for Tom, Dick and Harry, nobody got a bonus for Christmas.
7. Imhotep was the real "Father of Medicine."
8. Whenever fat is skinny, there will be no controversy.
9. Almost every one of the videos I rented from them is defective.
10. Tennis is an excellent exercise for those who can play it.
11. Unless you were in the know, you were left out of the mix.
12. Anything called rap music has got to be bad.
13. Only bells can be tolls, and only cymbals can cause alarms.
14. There are thieves around wherever there are crowds of people.
15. None of the previous Superbowls have been worth watching.
16. Every rat is a rodent.
17. Not every pet is a properly trained animal.
18. Alpha Alpha Greek is the only fraternity which can have campus parties.
19. Only Davids can be Pets and only Devins can be cute.
20. Anything that ugly qualifies as a monster.

CONVERSIONS OF CATEGORICAL CLAIMS

A great deal of the fascination with categorical claims is the convertibility of their terms. That is, in saying "All apples are Fruit" are we also saying "All Fruit are apples"? Of course not. Each of the four basic categorical statement patterns has its own rule(s) for conversion. (Refer back to the Venn diagrams to visually affirm this point.)

A-claims are not convertible. ("All A is P" cannot be converted into "all P is A.")

E-claims are convertible. ("No A is P" is exactly equivalent to "no P is A.")

I-claims are convertible. ("Some A is P" is exactly equivalent to "some P is A.")

O-claims cannot be converted. ("Some A is not P" is not equivalent to "some P is not A.")

Conversion essentially has to do with being able to exchange the subject and the predicate terms in categorical statements without fundamentally changing the original claim made. Thus, "All purple-people-eaters are greedy things," if converted becomes "All greedy things are purple-people-eaters" (A claim), which definitively changes the original claim. It is an improper conversion. For the four categories, students can remember that the two extremes (Alpha and Omega) cannot be converted, while the middles (Eta and Ita) can be.

THE SQUARE OF OPPOSITION

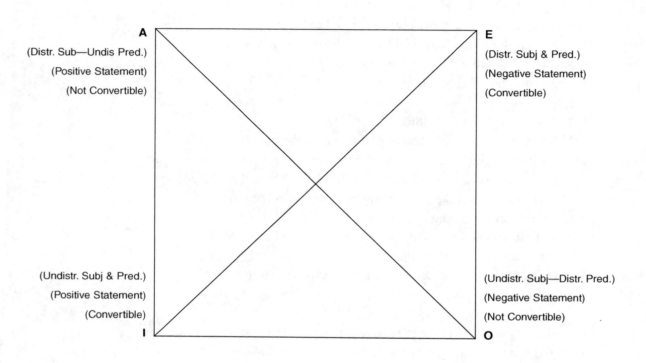

A
(Distr. Sub—Undis Pred.)
(Positive Statement)
(Not Convertible)

E
(Distr. Subj & Pred.)
(Negative Statement)
(Convertible)

(Undistr. Subj & Pred.)
(Positive Statement)
(Convertible)
I

(Undistr. Subj—Distr. Pred.)
(Negative Statement)
(Not Convertible)
O

CATEGORICAL SYLLOGISMS

A categorical syllogism is a two-premise deductive argument based on the four traditional categorical statements, containing no more than three terms, and in which those three terms each occur exactly twice in exactly two of the claims (i.e., twice in either of the two premises, or within one premise and the conclusion). Example: All cats are animals. Some animals are not wild things. Thus, some cats are not wild things.

The three terms are "cats," "animals," and "wild things." "Animals" is used in the two premises; "wild things" in the second premise and the conclusion; and "cats" and "wild things" are connected in the conclusion. The terms of a syllogism are traditionally labeled:

1. Major Term (term which is the predicate in the conclusion)
2. Minor Term (term which is the subject in the conclusion)
3. Middle Term (term which occurs in both premises but not in the conclusion)

EXAMPLES OF SYLLOGISMS AND PSEUDO-SYLLOGISMS

Syllogisms

All feathers are soft and fluffy quills.

No soft, fluffy quills are worth anything.

Therefore, no feathers are worth anything.

Peter is all wet

Those all wet are not sane.
Therefore, Peter is not sane.

(Remember to translate sentence #1
into an A-statement)

Nobody who is home can leave the house.
Those who can leave can see the mouse.
Therefore, nobody home can see the mouse.

Pseudo-Syllogisms

All feathers are soft and fluffy.

No feathers are also pretty.

Thus, soft and fluffy is sometimes not pretty.

Peter is all wet.

Peter is not sane.
Therefore, all wet.

Peter is not sane.
Peter.

Nobody who is home can leave the house.
Everybody who is home can see the mouse.
Therefore, everybody who can see the mouse can't leave the house.

TESTING FOR THE VALIDITY OF SYLLOGISMS

I. The Rules Method is based on two principles:

1. The four categorical statements represent two affirmative claims (A and I) and two negative claims (E and O).

2. Terms that occur in the premises and the conclusion are either distributed or not distributed (undistributed). Distribution here means that the claim says something about all members of a class represented by a term, in which case it is distributed, or it only says something about part (or some) of that class, in which case it is undistributed.

Three of the standard forms distribute either the subject or predicate terms (A, O), or both (E). One form distributes neither (I). The summation below demonstrates what is distributed (Bold Parenthesis) and what isn't.

A-statement   (All S) is P

E-statement   No (S) is (P)

I-statement   Some S are P

O-statement   Some S are not (P)

II. A categorical syllogism is valid only if all of the following five conditions are met:

1. At least one of the two premises must distribute the middle term.
2. The same number of negative claims made in the premises must be made in the conclusion. *Note:* This also means that no valid syllogism can have two negative premises, since the conclusion is only one claim.
3. Any term which is distributed in the conclusion must also be distributed in one of the premises.
4. Whenever one premise in a syllogism is an I statement, the other premise must be either an A or an E statement.
5. Terms in the conclusion, if converted, must follow the rules of proper conversion.

Apply the Rules of Syllogisms to each item. Determine whether each is a valid or invalid syllogism. If invalid, demonstrate which rule was broken.

1. All piano players are great hands people.
   But some great hands people are not decent baseball players.
   Therefore, all piano players are decent baseball players.

2. All Petes are Willies.
   No Willies are Richards.
   Thus, no Petes are Richards.

3. Some kittens are caterwaulers.
   Some caterwaulers are not chicken-feathered.
   So, some kittens are not chicken-feathered either.

4. All hats are in my hands.
   All in my hands are safe from harm.
   Thus, everything safe from harm is a hat.

5. No Millers are Great Lite Beers.
   Some Buds are not great Lites either.
   So, no Millers are some Buds.

6. No merry merchants are noble landlords.
   Although all merry merchants are bankers for real estate.
   Therefore, no real estate bankers are noble landlords.

7. Some dogs are smart animals.
   Some smart animals are not pretty animals.
   Some dogs are not pretty animals.

8. Dinosaurs, unless they are fakes, are all dead creatures and can never be alive again.

9. Mice carry lice.
   Lice carry germs.
   Mice, lice, and germs must go.

10. No one thing is always a good thing.
    All good things are sweet things.
    Some things are not sweet things.

THE VENN DIAGRAM METHOD

To diagram a syllogism to test its validity requires three overlapping circles, one representing each class named by a term in the argument. Put the circle for the minor term on the left, the major term on the right, and the middle term in the lower middle.

EXAMPLE

No Democratic Bullwinkles are Republican Consoles.
All fiscal tightwads are also Republican Consoles.
Therefore, no fiscal tightwads are Democratic Bullwinkles.

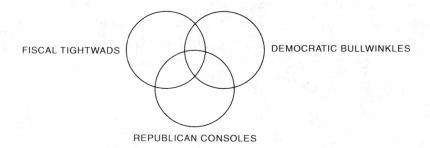

Fiscal tightwads is the minor term, Democratic Bullwinkles is the major term and Republican Consoles is the middle term. Remembering the diagramming of the A, E, I, O statement earlier in the Chapter, the following is how Venn diagrams are used, based on the six rules listed below. (Refer back to the beginning section on categoricals.)

1. Shaded areas (used with A and E claims) mean that part of the category is empty (where the circles don't overlap).
2. X's mean that part of two or more circles share the population of a category (always used with I and O claims).
3. When one premise is an A or E premise and the other is an I or O premise, diagram (shade) the A or E premise first.
4. A syllogism is valid if and only if correctly diagramming the premises automatically equals a correct diagram for the conclusion.
5. Whenever there is uncertainty about where to put an X after the other diagramming has been done, an X that can go in either of two areas will be placed on the line separating the areas. However, in order to produce the conclusion, ultimately the X has to be entirely in one area or another. If that cannot be done, then the syllogism is invalid.
6. The one exception to rule #4 is that whenever both premises are either A or E, and the conclusion is I or O, then correctly diagramming the premises can't lead directly to the conclusion. In this case, place an X in the circle area left unshaded, so in this example you would have both shaded areas and an X. Once this is done, if the diagram then produces the conclusion, the syllogism is valid. If it doesn't, then the syllogism is invalid.

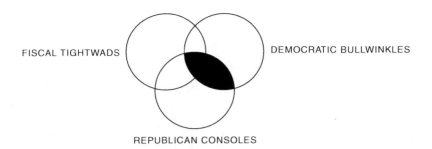

FIGURE A

No Democratic Bullwinkles are Republican Consoles.

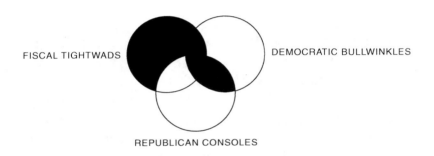

FIGURE A

No Democratic Bullwinkles are Republican Consoles.
All Fiscal Tightwads are also Republican Consoles.

With both premises diagrammed, the conclusion, no fiscal tightwads are Democratic Bullwinkles is self-evident (The circles to the left and to the right have only shaded areas between them, which means they share nothing).

ANOTHER EXAMPLE

1. Some Pollies are not Mollies. But all Gollies are Mollies. So, Some Pollies are not Gollies (*Note:* Diagram the A premise first.)

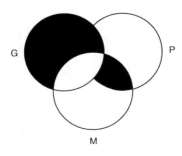

(1)

2. All Wots are Phigs. Some Luts are Phigs. So, Some Luts are Wots. (*Note:* Again, diagram the A premise first.)

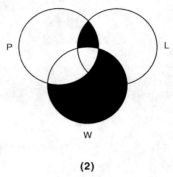

(2)

Figure D: Diagram the A-premise. The X, which is ambiguous (it can go in either of two areas) should be placed on the line separating those two areas.

The X on the line means we need more information to decide in which distinct area the I-statement subject term goes. However, more importantly, this diagram shows an invalid syllogism since the middle is undistributed (and students can tell that there is a problem with validity whenever they can't readily determine from the premise evidence given in exactly what area the X of an I or O statement will fall).

Note: As a rule of thumb, students will fare much better when they determine the validity or invalidity of a syllogism before they diagram it.

I. COMMON TYPES OF VALID AND INVALID ARGUMENTS

Some types of valid and invalid arguments occur so frequently that it makes sense to remember their patterns. In Parts I, II, and III such commonly occurring patterns are demonstrated.

1. Modus Ponens (affirming the antecedent)

Example:

If P then Q.

P.

Therefore, Q.

If John went home he is now in bed.

He did go home.

Therefore, he is now in bed.

2. Modus Tollens (denying the consequent)

Example:

If P then Q.

Not Q.

Therefore, not P.

If John went home, he is now in bed.

He is not in bed now.

Therefore, he didn't go home.

3. Chain argument

Example:

If P then Q.

If Q then R.

Therefore, if P then R.

If John went home, then he is in bed now.

If he is in bed now, then he is asleep.

Therefore, if John went home, he is sleep.

TWO COMMON INVALID PATTERNS

1. Affirming the consequent

Example:

If P then Q.

Q.

Therefore, P.

If John went home, he is in bed now.

He's in bed now

Therefore, John went home

2. Denying the antecedent

Example:

If P then Q.

Not P.

Therefore, not Q.

If John went home, he is in bed now.

John did not go home.

Therefore, he's not in bed now

II. COMMON TYPES OF VALID AND INVALID ARGUMENT PATTERNS

Valid Conversion 1:

No X's are Y's.

Therefore, no Y's are X's.

Example:

No polo players are club members.

Therefore, no members are polo players.

Valid Conversion 2:

Some X's are Y's.

Therefore, some Y's are X's.

Example:

Some polo players are club members.

Therefore, some members are players.

Here are some patterns which look very similar to those above but which are invalid:

Invalid Conversion 1:

All X's are Y's.

Therefore, all Y's are X's.

Example:

All polo players are members.

Therefore, all members are also polo players.

Invalid Conversion 2:

Some X's are not Y's.

Therefore, some Y's are not X's.

Example:

Some polo players are not members

Therefore, some members are not polo players.

One other form deserves special emphasis because it is so common:

Invalid Inference (Non Sequitur):

Some X's are Y's.

Therefore, some X's are not Y's.

Example:

Some polo players are members.

Therefore, some polo players are not members.

It is also not valid to run the last argument in reverse:

Some X's are not Y's

Therefore, some X's are Y's

Some polo players are not members

Therefore, some members are polo players.

Note: "Some" can, in reality, mean "all," so assuming it does not is invalid.

III. COMMON TYPES OF VALID AND INVALID SYLLOGISTIC ARGUMENTS

Valid Syllogism 1:

All X's are Y's.

All Y's are Z's.

Therefore all X's are Z's.

Example:

All polo players are great horsemen.

All great horsemen are gentle people of leisure.

Therefore, all polo players are gentle people of leisure.

Valid Syllogism 2:

All X's are Y's.

No Y's are Z's.

Therefore, no X's are Z's.

Example:

All polo players are great horsemen.

No great horsemen are gentle people of leisure.

Therefore, no polo players are gentle people of leisure.

Invalid Syllogism 1:

All X's are Y's.

No Z's are X's.

Therefore, no Y's are Z's.

Example:

All polo players are great horsemen.

No members are polo players.

Therefore, no great horsemen are members.

Are the following diagrams accurate reflections of the arguments given? Are the syllogisms valid or invalid?

1. No C are non-S.
   All non-S are B.
   No B are C.

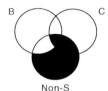

2. All T are E.
   All HT are E.
   All HT are T.

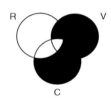

3. All H are S.
   No R are S.
   No R are H.

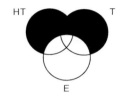

4. All C are R.
   All V are C.
   No R are V.

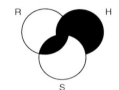

5. No empty disks that contain data.
   Some empty disks are formatted disks.
   Some formatted disks are not disks that contain data.

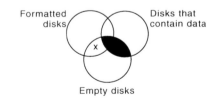

6. All products are substances damaging to people's health.
   Some pork products are high in cholesterol.
   Some high cholesterol substances are substances damaging to people's health.

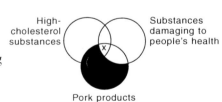

7. All people who may vote are citizens of the country.
   Mr. Hopkins is not a person who may vote.
   Mr. Hopkins is not a citizen of the country.

   Note: Remember that claims with individuals as subject terms are treated as A or E claims.

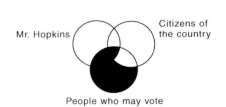

Identify whether the following are or are not proper syllogisms; whether they are valid or invalid; and if valid, draw the proper Venn diagram to reflect them.

1. Wee Willie Winkle has 310 sisters.
   Wee Willie also has 510 brothers.
   Thus, Wee Willie has 820 siblings.

2. All 50s are 100s.
   Some 100s are 1000s.
   So, some 50s are 1000s.

3. Jerry has 9 books with 18 stamps.
   The 18 stamps have 36 colored corners.
   Therefore, Jerry's 9 books have 4 (9) colored corners

4. No F's are G's.
   No G's are C's.
   So, No C's are G's.

5. Every brown boy was wings.
   Everybody with wings is golden.
   So, every brown baby is a nugget.

6. All 1s are 2s.
   All 2s are 4s.
   Therefore, All 1s are 4s.

7. All T's are Z's.
   But no Z's are X's.
   Therefore, No X's are T's.

8. Elected officials always tell the truth, so the real truth tellers always get elected so they can serve the public.

9. All F's are G's.
   This is a P and an F.
   Therefore, every F is a PG.

10. No Q's are not R's.
    Some babies are Q's.
    Therefore, some babies must not be R's.

11. Some purses can not be sow bellies.
    Yet some sow bellies can not be ham fat.
    Therefore, a lot of ham fat ain't purses.

12. Fools are foolish.
    Nobody foolish is crazy.
    Therefore, nobody crazy is a fool

13. Every one horse is never a riding mule.
    Every riding mule is never a thoroughbred.
    Therefore, a true thoroughbred is never one horse.

14. Licks are sticks.
    Licks are also picks.
    Therefore, every good pick is a very good lick!

15. Salami is always tasty.
    When it is tasty it's always rotten.
    All salami is always rotten, therefore.

16. Some like it hot.
    Some like it cold.
    Some like it both hot and cold.
    Therefore, some like it both hotcold or coldhot.

17. Liars never cheat, and Cheaters never Lie before they Die.
    So, it's your turn to Die if you don't Lie your Cheating
    Self out of it first.

18. All TV evangelists have high moral standards, and those with high morals all want to be TV
    evangelists to make a lot of money, but for the right reasons.

19. No Grates are Peels, so no Peels are Grates either.

20. When some chauvinists are real hairy pigs,
    we know for certain that some hairy pigs must be real chauvinists.

21. All O's are OO's.
    No O's are III's.
    Therefore, No OO's are III's.

22. All men are either sexists or liberals.
    No sexists or liberals are worth two pennies.
    So, no men are worth two pennies.

23. No 2s are 5s.
    But some 5s are 20s.
    So, some 2s are 20s.

24. No 20s are 30s.
    Although some 10s are 20s.
    So, some 10s are not 30s.

25. No corn has ears, unless it is ripe.
    Pim's corn is not ripe.
    So, it doesn't have ears.

CHAPTER SEVEN

FORMAL LOGIC CONTINUED: TRUTH TABLES, EQUIVALENCE, AND LOGICAL DERIVATIONS

Truth tables in logic use the information introduced in the previous chapter to establish the logical equivalence of statement claims, and to test a formal argument for validity. A truth table is a tabular chart of all the possible true and false values for the component parts of complex arguments. A complex argument is two or more simple claims and premises connected by "and," "or," or the "if-then" conditional, so that it frequently appears as a compound English sentence or sentences. Truth values do not mean truth per se, but rather because of the form (e.g., conjunction, disjunction) of the argument premises and claims, what will be the truth value (measured by true and false) of each component, and what are the applicable rules for the situation?

For example, below is a truth table for five types of connectives introduced on page 131 in Chapter 6. Note that the truth values are directly under the logical connectives.

XY	X & Y	X v Y	~X	X→B	X↔Y
TT	T	T	F	T	T
TF	F	T	F	F	F
FT	F	T	T	T	F
FF	F	F	T	T	T

This truth table shows the typical relationship of two variables identified in the first two columns on the left side, called index columns. Because there are only two variables, all the possible truth values for simple statement components of an argument which use the ampersand connective, the disjunctive vel or wedge, the tilda, the if-then conditional, and the biconditional are shown in four lines of the table. In other words, the table shows what each statement form would equal and is equivalent to (in relationship to) X and Y in a readily accessible, quick-glance arrangement.

If there were three variables in the index column, the truth table would have eight lines. If there were four variables, there would be sixteen lines, and so on. The formula for the number of lines in a truth table is simply 2^x = number of lines, where X equals the number of variables displayed. Thus 2^2=4 lines, 2^3=8 lines, 2^4=16 lines, and so on.

For those of you who are math-phobic, not to worry. The math of truth tables gets no more complicated than those simple exponent calculations.

It should be noted at the outset that truth tables simply represent a visual device for showing formal logical equivalence and validity. While truth tables can show such equivalence and can demonstrate the validity and invalidity of any formal logical argument, no matter how long or complicated, after a certain number of variables, generally four or five, truth tables can become unwieldy and very time-consuming unless one is using a computer.

In addition, the following rules for both equivalence and the analysis of validity and non-validity are reference points for the rest of the chapter.

CONJUNCTIONS (&)

Conjunctions are only true when both of their conjuncts are true. In all other cases, conjunctions have the truth value False.

T & T = T(rue)

T & F = F(alse)

F & T = F(alse)

F & F = F(alse)

DISJUNCTIONS (V)

Inclusive Disjunction	Exclusive Disjunction
T v T = T	T v T = F
T v F = T	T v F = T
F v T = T	F v T = T
F v F = F	F v F = F

In Inclusive (Standard) Disjunction (e.g., X v Y, or both) it is true when both of its disjuncts are true, and when either one of its disjuncts is true. It is false only when both of its disjuncts are false.

An Exclusive Disjunction (e.g., X v Y, but not both) on the other hand, which is specifically either this option or that one, but not both, has the truth value true only when either one or the other disjunct is true. When both disjuncts are true or both are false, then the truth value of the Exclusive Disjunction is false.

CONDITIONALS (→)

T→T = T

T→F = F

$F \rightarrow T = T$

$F \rightarrow F = T$

Conditionals are hypotheticals. They have the truth value of false only when the antecedent is true while the consequent simultaneously is false. In all other cases, conditionals have the truth value of true, including the curious situation of both the antecedent and the consequent being simultaneously false.

BICONDITIONALS (↔ or ≡)

A biconditional is, in fact, two conditional statements joined together so that the antecedent and the consequent of the first statement will become the consequent and antecedent of the second statement, respectively. The truth value of biconditionals is straightforward: they are true when both variables are the same (i.e., both true or both false) and false when the variables are different from each other.

$T \leftrightarrow T = T$

$T \leftrightarrow F = F$

$F \leftrightarrow T = F$

$F \leftrightarrow F = T$

NEGATIONS AND DOUBLE NEGATIONS (~)

Tildas are not binary connectives and thus do not connect two or more component parts of complex statements. Although they are unary symbols which only go in front of statements, they can create rather complex statement situations. At their simplest, tildas negate or contradict the original meaning of a logical statement so that the statement is translated as, "it is not the case that." Tildas cause statements to have the truth value that is directly opposite their original truth value. Essentially, this equates to the negation of a true statement equaling a false statement, and the negation of a false statement equaling a true statement.

$\sim T = F$ $\sim \sim \sim T = F$

$\sim F = T$ $\sim \sim \sim F = T$

$\sim \sim T = T$

$\sim \sim F = F$

Every two negatives, or tildas, cancel themselves, so that an even number of tildas in front of a statement affirms the statement and an odd number of tildas negates the statement.

GROUPING, FOR STATEMENTS WITH MULTIPLE CONNECTIVES

To better handle situations in which statements have two or more binary connectives and two or more sentences, group the symbolic statements into parentheses and brackets. No more than two symbolic variables should appear with a binary connective within each specific parenthesis, and a tilda may be inside or outside the parenthesis or bracket. Tildas inside and outside the parenthesis mean entirely different things and each should be carefully scrutinized before trying to translate or convert such logical statements.

EXAMPLES:

(~X→Y)   = ~(X→Y)

If not X, then Y   It is false that if X, then Y.

DETERMINING LOGICAL EQUIVALENCE IN TRUTH TABLES

Two statements are logically equivalent only when their truth table values are exactly the same. Example, "Put your hands in the air right now or I'll be forced to hurt you!" and "If you don't put your hands in the air right now, I'll be forced to hurt you!" Let HA = Hands in the air, and FH = forced to hurt you.

HA	FH	HA v FH	~HA→FH	
T	T	T	F	T
T	F	T	F	F
F	T	T	T	T
F	F	F	T	F

HA	FH	HA v FH	~HA→FH
T	T	T	T
T	F	T	T
F	T	T	T
F	F	F	F

Thus, the two statements are logically equivalent. They are equally true on lines 1–3 and false on line 4. Their truth values match.

SOLUTION STEPS

    a. Construction of the truth values for HA v FH is based on the rules for an inclusive disjunction, either . . . or, or both. In that regard, all the truth values are true except when both disjuncts are false.

    b. For ~HA, the values must be an exact opposite to those for HA, and those for FH are simply repeated from the index column.

    c. The truth values under the conditional arrow are based on the principle that the conditional is false only when the antecedent is true and the consequent is false.

    d. To eliminate confusion, circle the final truth values and cross or lineout the initial ones not in the index column. Make sure that the final truth values are directly under the main connective of each expression, in this case the v and the →.

These steps are typical in constructing a truth table. The following are additional "givens" for equivalences in truth tables.

1. There are always at least 3 possible placements for tildas to be concerned with in complex (compound) logical statements: in front of either of the symbolic variables, or it may be placed in front of a parenthesis or bracket of symbols connected by an ampersand, wedge, or arrow. Call the first placement option Tilda I, the second Tilda II, and the third Tilda III.

2. Disjunctions can be restated as conditionals, and conditionals restated as disjunctions. Most frequently, in order to maintain the equivalence between the two expressions, the rule is, negate only the symbol in the first position (either the antecedent or the first disjunct, depending on which is being converted to what).

    Thus, the following statements are given equivalents:

    ~A v ~B = A→B

    A v ~B = ~A→ ~B

    ~(A v B) = ~(~A→B)

    In every case, note that only the A changes from negative to positive, or positive to negative.

3. Conjunctions can be rewritten as disjunctions, but only if all three tilda options are utilized.

    Thus, the following equivalences:

    A v B = + ~(~A & ~B)

    ~A v B = ~(A & ~B)

    ~(A v ~B) = ~A & B

4. Conjunctions can also be changed to conditionals. Here, the rule is: change Tilda II and Tilda III, but not Tilda I.

    Thus, the equivalences are:

$$A \rightarrow \sim B = (A \& B)$$

$$\sim(A \rightarrow B) = A \& \sim B$$

$$\sim A \rightarrow B = \sim(\sim A \& \sim W)$$

As an efficient way to remember all of this, logicians typically utilize a Conversion Pyramid, as shown below.

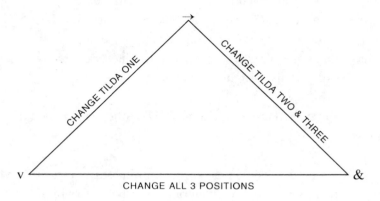

EXERCISE A

Construct truth tables and determine whether the following logical statements are equivalent or not. Make sure to follow the steps and rules as provided in the Chapter.

1. $\sim(A \vee \sim C)$ and $A \rightarrow C$
2. $E \vee \sim F$ and $E \rightarrow \sim F$
3. $\sim P \& Q$ and $P \rightarrow Q$
4. $A \rightarrow \sim D$ and $\sim A \vee \sim D$
5. $\sim(B \rightarrow T)$ and $B \& T$
6. $A \rightarrow Y$ and $\sim(\sim A \& \sim Y)$
7. The river is flowing and the fish are swimming, and whenever the river flows, then the fish swim.
8. Either Donner or Blizten will make this trip, and Donner and Blizten won't both make this trip.
9. $A \vee W = \sim A \rightarrow W$
10. $\sim X \vee \sim Y = X \rightarrow \sim Y$
11. Give me your money or I'll jump overboard, and if you give me your money, I won't have to jump overboard.
12. If peas don't pop, then Curtis can't rock. Either peas will pop, or Curtis can't rock.
13. Either I will graduate, or Peter won't. If I don't graduate, then Peter won't.
14. $\sim(L \rightarrow M) + \sim L \rightarrow \sim M$
15. Pigs and cows, and either pigs or cows.

TRUTH TABLES AND ARGUMENT VALIDITY

In formal and informal logic, valid deductive arguments are those in which the conclusion is made mandatory (or is compelled) by the evidentiary premises. Another way commonly used in logic to say the same thing is that the logical truth (not necessarily factual truth) of a deductive argument's premises guarantees the logical truth of the conclusion. It is also the case that logically false premises must lead to a logically false conclusion in order to be valid.

Truth tables provide one visual means of measuring the validity or invalidity of deductive arguments based on the argument's premises and conclusions fitting the prescribed statement forms already discussed (i.e., disjunctions, conjunctions, etc.). Below, the process is described.

SEQUENTIAL STEPS IN THE PROCESS

1. Although the rules are specific for each form, the basic truth table format is the same for disjunctions, conditionals, conjunctions, etc. List in the left-side index column the letter variables in the argument under review.

EXAMPLE

R   B   B

Either a <u>red coat</u> or a <u>blue one</u> will do, but I don't have a <u>blue coat</u>, so I guess it'll have to be the

R

<u>red one</u>.

Remember the rules discussed previously: Two variables equal four lines, three variables equal eight, and so on. The basic pattern of initial truth value combinations for the index column is standard.

R v B	R	B
~B	T	T
R	T	T
	F	T
	F	T

Remember the rules discussed previously: Two variables equal four lines, three variables equal eight, and so on. The basic pattern of initial truth value combinations for the index column is standard.

2. Add the symbolic lettered premises across the top of the table in separate columns, and the conclusion in the last column of the table. Add the relevant truth values associated with the connectives which are part of the argument (see the first part of the chapter.)

	R	B	R v B	~B	R
1.	T	T	T	F	T
2.	T	F	T	T	T
3.	F	T	T	F	F
4.	F	F	F	T	F

3. Review the lines within the table to ensure compliance with the rule: In truth tables, there cannot be any lines in which all of the premises have the value True and the conclusion has the truth value False, if the argument under review is valid. Arguments with the pattern "all premises True, conclusion false," are invalid.

Thus, the example under review is a valid disjunction argument. Line 2, the only line in which both premises have the value True, has a corresponding conclusion with a value True. Lines 1, 3 and 4 do not have all premises with the value True and are not relevant in this analysis.

OTHER EXAMPLES

$P \rightarrow Q$

Q

P

	P	Q	P→Q	Q	P
1.	T	T	T	T	T
2.	T	F	T	F	T
3.	F	T	T	T	F
4.	F	F	F	F	F

Line (1) complies with the rule for validity; line (3) does not. The argument is thus invalid. What argument form is this?

$Y \rightarrow X$

$X \rightarrow ZA$

$\underline{\sim Y}$

$\sim ZA$

	Y	X	ZA	Y→Q	X→ZA	~Y	~ZA
1.	T	T	T	T	T	F	F
2.	T	T	F	T	F	F	T
3.	T	F	T	F	T	F	F
4.	T	F	F	F	F	,F	T
5.	F	T	T	T	T	T	F
6.	F	T	F	T	F	T	T
7.	F	F	T	T	T	T	F
8.	F	F	F	T	T	T	T

Line (8) complies with the rule for validity, but lines (7) and (5) do not. Thus, this argument is invalid. What type of argument is it?

LOGICAL DERIVATION PROOFS

The most efficient alternative to truth tables for assessing validity/non-validity in formal logic is derivation proofs. D.P.'s are based on combining evidentiary premises and logical rules in order to arrive at logical statements and positions. In other words, derivation proofs represent logical analysis from premises and rules to conclusions. There are logical rules for combining statements together, for separating them, and for deriving seemingly new information from those combinations and separations. In fact, the "new" information was already implicit within the evidentiary premises and rules, and merely needed logical analysis/combination to bring the "new" information out in the open. This is what Sherlock Holmes made famous, and is the same process practiced by numerous investigators, detectives, inspectors, researchers, and puzzle games enthusiasts. Essentially, one "solves" logical problems by deriving a conclusion through several integrated steps or moves, or put another way, one wins a logical game by determining whether one can validly arrive at a conclusion compelled by the combination of related evidence.

EXAMPLE:

a. Determine the validity of ~DT = BB in the following:

$$\text{CB} \qquad\qquad\qquad \text{BB}$$

The <u>Chicago Bulls with M. Jordan</u> is the <u>best Basketball Team in history</u>, or <u>it can't be</u>

$$\quad\text{~DT} \qquad\qquad\qquad \text{~QT}$$

<u>determined which team was</u> the best. And if <u>the quality of the opposing teams</u> in various eras

$$\qquad\qquad\qquad\qquad\qquad \text{~DT}$$

can't be measured in some objective and tangible way, then certainly <u>it can't be determined</u>

CB   ~QT

whether the <u>Jordan Bulls Team</u> is the best <u>or not</u>. Well, even in this modern age, <u>there doesn't</u>

<u>seem to be</u> such a <u>tangible</u>, non-subjective way.

D.P. STEPS

1. (CB v ~DT) & ~(CB & ~DT) = BB (Exclusive DA)

   ~QT→ ~DT

   <u>~QT</u>

   ~DT

   .:. ~CB and ~DT = BB

2. As an Exclusive Disjunction Argument, this means either the Bulls Team is the best or it can't be determined, but not both of them. This is the exception to the regular DA rule for validity.
3. The Modus Ponens argument of the 2nd, 3rd and 4th premises yields the conclusion that since it can't be determined (~DT) then the Jordan Bulls cannot be the best (~CB), based on the rules for m.p. arguments.
4. Thus, it can't be determined (~DT) which team is the best in basketball (BB).

D.P. GOAL

The latter, ~DT = BB was the conclusion to be proven valid or invalid. Here, it is valid and compelled by the combination of statements and rules.

This robe is either red or black. But if it's from Pakistan, it surely can't be black, and, according to the lapel, it was make nowhere else but Pakistan.

1. R v B

2. P→ ~B

3. <u>P   </u>

4. ~B

5. .:. R

Line four, the intermediate conclusion, is derived from a modus ponens argument form shown in lines 2 and 3. Line 5 is logically derived from lines 4 and 1, following the logical rules for the non-exclusive disjunctive argument.

A.

Determine the validity or invalidity of the following arguments by using a truth table for each of them.

1. Life is only about dying, slowly or with some speed. If it is slow, then the road is tortuous and bumpy. If it is with speed, it is yet tortuous and bumpy. Thus, life and dying shall be tortuous and bumpy.

2. If David does not go, then Shanda will not either. Well, Shanda is definitely going, so David will therefore go too.

3. If the chickens must come home to roost, then the scuttlebutt will surely fly. The chickens are home roosting now, so get ready for the scuttlebutt!

4. Whenever I'm sad and depressed, the sun always shines all day. I'm sad and depressed right now, so the sun will surely shine bright all day.

5. If I hate you, then I know somebody will get hurt. But if you hate me, somebody will still get hurt. So either way it goes, hate is going to get somebody hurt.

6. Either you are rich and successful, or you're poor and ugly. You sure don't look rich and famous to me. You know the rest, right?

7. If you ride the great horse to Nantucket, you will gain the Holy Grail. And if you get the Holy Grail, then you are the next emperor of this great land. So, you will either be the emperor or a non-rider.

8. Charles is either going to Harvard or Yale. If he goes to Harvard, then Susan must go to Stanford. If he goes to Yale, then Ralph must stay home. So either Charles helps Susan go to Stanford or he makes Ralph stay home.

9. If Africa is the birthplace of mankind, then we are all Africans. If Africa wasn't, then we don't know where we all come from. So if we didn't come from Africa, are we from outer space?

10. Either X or Y. If Z, no X. If no X, then the Y's have it. There is no Z.

B.

Use a Derivative Proof method to find the logical conclusions to the following, and state the rules in your analysis.

1. CA→BT

   BT→P

   ~P

   ∴ ~CA

2. Doppleblut or Whistlerow.
   If not Whistlerow, then no fish.
   There is no Whistlerow.
   Therefore, there is no Doppleblut.

3. V→W

   V v Z

   ~Z

   .:. W

4. ~(L & P)

   L

   M→P

   .:. ~M

5. A v B

   B→C

   A→C

   C→F

   .:. F

CHAPTER EIGHT

LOGIC IN EVERDAY LIFE

I. FORMAL LOGIC

As described in Chapters 6 and 7, Formal Logic is highly useful in debate tournaments, in solving games and puzzles, in handling standardized test questions, and, in its less complicated forms, essay writing and communication reasoning. Essentially, however, in its broadest sense, Formal Logic is too often an esoteric, abstract academic exercise divorced from real life, except for computer programming and other such activities.

In fact, Formal Logic is the language milieu of computers. Programmers of the 1980s and 1990s, software specialists, and virtually anyone who worked in COBOL, Pascal, Basic, Prolog, and any number of formerly new and specific computer vocabularies, including Home Pages and Web Sites, and Integrated Communications Systems, all worked within the purview of modern symbolic logic. Those who followed into the digital age continued along, and further expanded, that same path. To be sure, all or even most of these practitioners of virtual world and cyberspace logic may not have been trained through symbolic logic courses, nor even through complementary advanced math courses. However, the universal computer environments within which they work is and will continue to be formal and symbolic logic (a.k.a., fuzzy logic and other epithets), whether booting DOS or surfing the Net in old-school ways, programming and learning the latest versions of Windows or Mac, researching artificial intelligence, or playing computer games. Software designers, programmers and hackers are the unofficial ambassadors of real-world Formal Logic. For computers in the future, including space travel and artificial intelligence, the prognostication is for more of the same. For computer users, however, common sense is far more important than Formal Logic.

II. INFORMAL LOGIC

Informal Logic, as emphasized in this text, has many valuable uses in everyday life. First, Informal Logic is a primary vehicle for critical thinking analysis, critiques, evaluation and assessments of everyday information. Chapters 2, 4, and 5 have already covered that ground in an introductory fashion.

Informal Logic (often in conjunction with elements of Formal Logic) is also important in the following selected everyday uses:

    a. Standardized Test-Taking
    b. Legal Reasoning
    c. Public Policy Analysis
    d. Essay Writing
    e. Scientific Reasoning
    f. Philosophical and Moral Reasoning
    g. Games, Puzzles, and Teasers
    h. Conversational Clarity

The following pages will provide examples of A–D for demonstration purposes.

STANDARDIZED TEST-TAKING

Logical Analysis questions, in one fashion or another, are regular features of standardized exams. Reading Comprehension questions, verbal analogies, data sufficiency, items relationships, and causal inferences are the most usual format for informal logical challenges. (see Figure VIII-1A)

    Students who wish to prepare themselves well for such exams—or even for college/university classroom exams—are strongly encouraged to finish at least one course in critical thinking skills and/or Introduction to Logic, the latter which must emphasize both informal deduction and formal, rather than just the latter.

FIGURE 8-1A: SAMPLE STANDARDIZED TEST QUESTIONS
FOR DEMONSTRATING THE APPLICATION OF INFORMAL AND FORMAL LOGIC

A traveling salesperson plans to visit each of six cities, which we shall designate A, B, C, D, E, F, once and only once during this selling season. In getting the visitation schedule together, the following restriction had to be observed:

    a. The salesperson could only visit D after having visited both C and E.
    b. The salesperson cannot visit E before A.
    c. The second city to be visited by the salesperson must be B.

  1. Which of the following could be the order in which the salesperson visits the six cities?
    a. A, B, E, C, F, D
    b. B, A, C, E, D, F
    c. F, B, D, C, A, E
    d. C, B, F, E, D, A
    e. D, B, E, A, C, F

  2. Which of the following must be true of the salesperson's visitation schedule?
    a. Visits A before C
    b. Visits B before D
    c. Visits B before F

d. Visits D before A

e. Visits E before C

3. If the salesperson visits F first, then which city could be visited third?

    I. A

   II. C

  III. D

    a. I only

    b. III only

    c. I and II only

    d. II and III only

    e. I, II, and III only

4. If the salesperson visits A immediately after F and immediately before E, then she must visit C

    a. First

    b. Third

    c. Fourth

    d. Fifth

    e. Sixth

5. Which of the following could be true of the salesperson's schedule?

    a. Visits A first

    b. Visits B first

    c. Visits C sixth

    d. Visits D fourth

    e. Visits E sixth

6. The salesperson visits F last. Which of the following could be the first and third cities on the schedule?

    a. A

    b. C

    c. D

    d. E

    e. F

7. If the salesperson visits F last, which of the following could be the first and third cities on the schedule?

    a. A and C

    b. A and F

    c. C and E

    d. C and F

    e. E and A

At an innovative health club, at the reception counter are four small lights, coordinated so that they are side by side and numbered sequentially one through four from left to right. The lights are part of the club's idea of customer-centered décor, and they signal individual fitness consultants for customers with appointment times. Tonight, five of the club's best fitness experts are on duty: Dennis, Floyd, Min, Lon, and Zeus.

> In order to signal Dennis, all four light flash.
> In order to signal Floyd, lights one and two flash.
> In order to signal Min, light one flashes alone.
> In order to signal Lon, lights two, three and four flash.
> In order to signal Zeus, lights three and four flash.

8. If lights two and three are off at the same time, then the fitness consultant signaled is
   a. Dennis
   b. Floyd
   c. Min
   d. Lon
   e. Zeus

9. If only lights one, three, and four are flashing, then which of the following consultants could be called?
   I. Dennis
   II. Lon
   III. Zeus
   IV. Min

   a. I only
   b. III and IV only
   c. I and II only
   d. II and III only
   e. I, II, III and IV

10. If light one is not flashing, then which of the following consultants could be signaled?
   I. Floyd
   II. Lon
   III. Zeus

   a. I only
   b. I and II only
   c. I , III only
   d. II and III only
   e. I, II and III

11. If light three is flashing and light two is off, then the consultant signaled is
    a. Dennis
    b. Floyd
    c. Min
    d. Lon
    e. Zeus

Mr. True Blues Band is scheduled to play six numbers during its evening set. We call the song numbers, J, K, L, M, N, and O. Each song will be played exactly one time during the set. The order in which the songs will be played is contingent on the following:

The N song must be played before both the J and the O songs
The M song must be played only after the J song
The K song must be the third number played

12. Which of the following can be the order in which the songs are played?
    a. Songs K, L, N, O, M, J
    b. Songs K, O, N, J, M. L
    c. Songs M, J, K, O, L, N
    d. Songs N, L, K, J, O, M
    e. Songs N, O, J, M, K, L

13. Which of the following must be true of the song order?
    a. Song L is played after K
    b. Song M is played after N
    c. Song N is played after K
    d. Song O is played after M
    e. Song O is played after J

14. Which of the following could be true of the song order?
    a. Song J is played sixth
    b. Song K is played first
    c. Song M is played second
    d. Song O is played sixth
    e. Song N is played third

15. If Mr. True Blues Band plays song L first, then which song must be played second?
    a. Song J
    b. Song K
    c. Song O
    d. Song M
    e. Song N

16. If Mr. True Blues Band plays song M immediately after it plays song L, and right before it plays song O, then song J must logically be played
    a. First
    b. Second
    c. Fourth
    d. Fifth
    e. Sixth

17. If Mr. True Blues Band plays song L sixth in the order, then which of the following could be both the first and second songs played?
    I. Songs N and J
    II. Songs N and O
    III. J and O

    a. I only
    b. II only
    c. I and II only
    d. I and III only
    e. I, II and III only

18. All of the following songs could be played immediately after song K except
    a. Song J
    b. Song L
    c. Song O
    d. Song N
    e. Song M

(ANSWERS: 1–a; 2–b; 3–c; 4–a; 5–a; 6–c; 7–a; 8–c; 9–b; 10–d; 11–e; 12–d; 13–b; 14–d; 15–e; 16–b; 17–c; 18–d)

LEGAL REASONING

In a mechanical description, legal reasoning is the process of arriving at a legal decision. It is always dependent upon a question of law related to a question of fact. The case, in the U.S., will either be a civil or criminal tribunal in which the burden of proof will be on the state or on the plaintiff to prove the accusation made. In civil cases, the burden of proof may shift back and forth between the accuser (plaintiff) and the accused (defendant), but in criminal cases the defendant does not usually have to prove innocence, only a "reasonable doubt" that he or she is guilty. The burden of proof in criminal cases stays with the prosecutor to show guilt by a preponderance of the evidence. Since in real life, court cases are rarely a clear-cut matter simply of the determination of the applicable law or regulation and whether, in fact, the accused violated that law and should be punished, there are several common factors which usually intervene into the equation. These include the frequent vagueness of relevant laws, statutes, or regulations; the strong influence of public taste, cultural perception, regional bias and interpretation when the rules and the facts are not absolutely clear; the common-law tradition of English and American law, which respects consistency with prior decisions; and conflicts in the testimony and other evidence used to establish the "facts" of the case.

Given all this, and the rule that cases must be decided one way or another—including dismissal, which is a triumph for the defendant—legal reasoning is anything but simple and straightforward.

The bulk of legal reasoning—arguments to support or refute claims, establish and discredit evidence, conclusively demonstrate one's position while simultaneously thrashing that of your opponent—is analogical. That is, the principle aim of the presentations is to show why the court should favor one set of case precedents over another. Legal reasoning utilizes virtually every aspect of informal deductive processes, and anything else ethical which may tip the scales in one or another client's favor.

Below are two classic U.S. Supreme Court case summaries, demonstrating much of what is important in logically arguing for a legal remedy.

PLESSY V. FERGUSON, 163 U.S. 537, 1896

Mr. Justice Brown delivered the opinion of the Court.

This case turns upon the constitutionality of an act of the general assembly of the state of Louisiana, passed in 1890, providing for separate railway carriages for the white and colored races.

The 1st section of the statue enacts "that all railway companies carrying passengers in their coaches in this state shall provide equal but separate accommodations for the white and colored races by providing two or more passenger coaches for each passenger train, or by dividing the passenger coaches by a partition so as to secure separate accommodations: *Provided,* that this section shall not be construed to apply to street railroads. No person or persons shall be permitted to occupy seats in coaches other than the ones assigned to them, on account of the race they belong to."

By the 2nd section it was enacted "that the officer of such passenger trains shall have the power and are hereby required to assign each passenger to the coach or compartment used for the race to which such passenger belongs; any passenger insisting on going into a coach or compartment to which by race he does not belong, shall be liable to a fine of $25 or in lieu thereof to imprisonment for a period of not more than twenty days in the parish prison; and should any passenger refuse to occupy the coach or compartment to which he or she is assigned by the officer of such railway, said officer shall have power to refuse to carry such passenger on his train, and for such refusal neither he nor the railway company which he represents shall be liable for damages in any of the courts of this state . . ."

The information filed in the criminal district court charged in substance that Plessy, being a passenger between two stations within the state of Louisiana, was assigned by officers of the company to the coach used for the race to which he belonged, but he insisted upon going into a coach used by the race to which he did not belong. Neither in the information nor plea was his particular race or color averred.

The petition for the writ of prohibition averred that petitioner was seven-eighths Caucasian and one-eighth African blood; that the mixture of colored blood was not discernible in him, and that he was entitled to every right, privilege, and immunity secured to citizens of the United States of the white race; and that, upon such theory, he took possession of a vacant seat in a coach where passengers of the white race were accommodated, and was ordered by the conductor to vacate said coach and take a seat in another assigned to persons of the colored race, and having refused to comply with such demand he was forcibly ejected with the aid of a police officer, and imprisoned in the parish jail to answer a charge of having violated the above act.

The constitutionality of this act is attacked upon the ground that it conflicts both with the 13th Amendment of the Constitution, abolishing slavery, and the 14th Amendment, which prohibits certain restrictive legislation on the part of the states.

1. That it does not conflict with the 13th Amendment, which abolished slavery and involuntary servitude, except as a punishment for crime, is too clear for argument . . .

. . . Indeed, we do not understand that the 13th Amendment is strenuously relied upon by the plaintiff in error in this connection.

2. By the 14th Amendment, all persons born or naturalized in the United States, and subject to the jurisdiction thereof, are made citizens of the United States and of the state wherein they reside; and the states are forbidden from making or enforcing any law which shall abridge the privileges or immunities of citizens of the United States, or shall deprive any person within their jurisdiction of the equal protection of the laws . . .

The object of the amendment was undoubtedly to enforce the absolute equality of the two races before the law, but in the nature of things it could not have been distinguished from political, equality, or a commingling of the two races upon terms unsatisfactory to either. Laws permitting, and even requiring their separation in places where they are liable to be brought into contact do not necessarily imply the inferiority of either race to the other, and have been generally, if not universally, recognized as within competency of the state legislatures in the exercise of their police power. The most common instance of this is connected with the establishment of separate schools for white and colored children, which have been held to be a valid exercise of the legislative power even by courts of states where the political rights of the colored race have been longest and most earnestly enforced . . .

[Justice Brown next reviews a whole series of cases where statues similar to the one in question have been upheld as constitutional.]

It is . . . suggested by the learned counsel for the plaintiff in error that the same argument that will justify the state legislature in requiring railways to provide separate accommodations for the two races will also authorize them to require separate cars to be provided for people whose hair is of a certain color, or who are aliens, or who belong to certain nationalities, or to enact laws requiring colored people to walk upon one side of the street, and white people upon the other, or requiring white men's houses to be painted white, and colored men's black, or their vehicles or business signs to be of different colors, upon the theory that one side of the street is as good as the other, or that a house or vehicle of one color is as good as one of another color. The reply to all this is that every exercise of the police power must be reasonable, and extend only to such laws as are enacted in good faith for the promotion of the public good, and not for the annoyance or oppression of a particular class. Thus in Yick Wo v. Hopkins it was held by this court that a municipal ordinance of the city of San Francisco to regulate the carrying on of public laundries within the limits of the municipality violated the provisions of the Constitution of the United States if it conferred upon the municipal authorities arbitrary power, at their own will, and without regard to discretion, in the legal sense of the term, to give or withhold consent as to persons or places, without regard to the competency of the persons applying, or the propriety of the places selected for the carrying on of the business. It was held to be a covert attempt on the part of the municipality to make an arbitrary and unjust discrimination against the Chinese race. While this was the case of a municipal ordinance a like principle has been held to apply to acts of a state legislature passed in the exercise of the police power.

So far, then, as a conflict with the 14th Amendment is concerned, the case reduces itself to the question whether the statute of Louisiana is a reasonable regulation, and with respect to this there necessarily be a large discretion on the part of the legislature. In determining the question of reasonableness it is at liberty to act with reference to the established usages, customs, and traditions of the people, and with a view to the promotion of their comfort, and the preservation of the public peace and good order. Gauged by this standard, we cannot say that a law which authorizes or even requires the separation of the two races in public conveyances is unreasonable or more obnoxious to the 14th Amendment than the acts of Congress requiring separate schools for colored children in the District of Columbia, the constitutionality of which does not seem to have been questioned, or the corresponding acts of state legislatures.

We consider the underlying fallacy of the plaintiff's argument to consist in the assumption that the enforced separation of the two races stamps the colored race with a badge of inferiority. If this be so, it is not by reason of anything found in the act, but solely because the colored race chooses to put that construction upon it. The argument necessarily assumes that if, as has been more than once the case, and is not unlikely to be so again, the colored race should become the dominant power in the state legislature, and should enact a law in precisely similar terms, it would thereby relegate the white race to an inferior position. We imagine that the white race, at least, would not acquiesce in this assumption. The argument also assumes that social prejudices may be overcome by legislation, and that equal rights cannot be secured to the negro except by an enforced commingling of the two races. We cannot accept this proposition. If the two races are to meet on terms of social equality, it must be the result of natural affinity, a mutual appreciation of each other's merits and a voluntary consent of individuals. As was said by the court of appeals of New York in People v. Gallagher, this end can neither be accomplished nor promoted by laws which conflict with the general sentiment of the community upon whom they are designed to operate. When the government, therefore, has secured to each of its citizens equal rights before the law and equal opportunities for improvement and adoption of the Fourteenth Amendment in 1868, it covered exhaustively consideration of the Amendment in Congress, ratification by the states, then existing practices in racial segregation, and the views of proponents and opponents of the Amendment. This discussion and our own investigation convinces us that, although these sources cast some light, it is not enough to resolve the problem with which we are faced. At best, they are inconclusive. The most avid proponents of the post-War Amendments undoubtedly intended them to remove all legal distinctions among "all persons born or naturalized in the United States." Their opponents, just as certainly, were antagonistic to both the letter and the spirit of the Amendments and wished them to have the most limited effect. What others in Congress and the state legislatures had in mind cannot be determined with any degree of certainty.

An additional reason for the inconclusive nature of the Amendment's history, with respect to segregated schools, is the status of public education at that time. In the South, the movement toward free schools, supported by general taxation, had not yet taken hold. Education of white children was largely in the hands of private groups. Education of Negroes was almost non-existent, and practically all of the race were illiterate. In fact, any education of Negroes was forbidden by law in some states. Today, in contrast, many Negroes have achieved outstanding success in the arts and sciences as well as in the business and professional world. It is true that public school education at the time of the Amendment on Northern States was generally ignored in the congressional debates. Even in the North, the conditions of public education did not approximate those existing today. The curriculum was usually rudimentary; ungraded schools were common in rural areas; the school term was but virtually unknown. As a consequence, it is not surprising that there should be so little in the history of the Fourteenth Amendment relating to its intended effect on the public education.

In the first cases in this Court construing the Fourteenth Amendment, decided shortly after its adoption, the Court interpreted it as proscribing all state-imposed discriminations against the Negro race. The doctrine of "separate but equal" did not make its appearance in this Court until 1896 in the case of Plessy v. Ferguson involving not education but transportation. American courts have since labored with the doctrine for over half a century . . .

. . . We come then to the question presented: Does segregation of children in public schools solely on the basis of race, even though the physical facilities and other "tangible" factors may be equal, deprive the children of the minority group of equal educational opportunities? We believe that it does.

In Sweatt v. Painter, in finding that a segregated law school for Negroes could not provide them equal educational opportunities, this Court relied in large part on "those qualities which are incapable of objective measurement but which make for greatness in a law school." In McLaurin v. Oklahoma State Regents, it has accomplished and performed all of the functions respecting social advantages with which it is endowed. Legislature is powerless to eradicate racial instincts or to abolish distinctions based upon physical differences, and the attempt to do so can only result in accentuating the difficulties of the present situation. If the civil and political rights of both races be equal, one cannot be inferior to the other civilly or politically. If one race be inferior to the other socially, the Constitution of the United States cannot put them upon the same plane . . .

The judgment of the court below is therefore affirmed.

BROWN V. BOARD OF EDUCATION, TOPEKA, KANSAS, 347, U.S. 483, 1954

Mr. Chief Justice Warren delivered the opinion of the Court.

These cases come to us from the States of Kansas, South Carolina, Virginia, and Delaware. They are premised on different facts and different local conditions, but a common legal question justifies their consideration together in this consolidated opinion.

In each of the cases, minors of the Negro race, through their legal representatives, seek the aid of the courts in obtaining admission to the public schools of their community on a non-segregated basis. In each instance, they had been denied admission to schools attended by white children under laws requiring or permitting segregation according to race. This segregation was alleged to deprive the plaintiffs of the equal protection of the laws under the Fourteenth Amendment. In each of the cases other than the Delaware case, a three-judge federal district court denied relief to the plaintiffs on the so-called "separate but equal" doctrine announced by this Court in Plessy v. Ferguson. Under the doctrine, equality of treatment is accorded then the races are provided substantially equal facilities, even though these facilities be separate. In the Delaware case, the Supreme Court of Delaware adhered to that doctrine, but ordered that the plaintiffs be admitted to the white schools because of their superiority to the Negro schools.

The plaintiffs contend that segregated public schools are not "equal" and cannot be made "equal," and that hence they are deprived of the equal protection of the laws. Because of the obvious importance of the question presented, the Court took jurisdiction. Argument was heard in the 1952 Term, and the reargument was heard this Term on certain questions propounded by the Court.

Reargument was largely devoted to the circumstances surrounding the Court, in requiring that a Negro admitted to a white graduate school be treated like all other students, again resorted to intangible considerations: " . . . his ability to study, to engage in discussions and exchange views with other students, and in general, to learn his profession." Such consideration applies with added force to children in grade and high schools. To separate them from others of similar age and qualifications solely because of their race generates a feeling of inferiority as to their status in the community that may affect their hearts and minds in a way unlikely ever to be undone. The effect of this separation on their educational opportunities was well stated by the finding in the Kansas case by a court which nevertheless felt compelled to rule against the Negro plaintiffs.

"Segregation of white and colored children in public schools has a detrimental effect upon the colored children. The impact is greater when it has the sanction of the law; for the policy of separating the races in usually interpreted as denoting the inferiority of the negro group. A sense of inferiority affects the motivation of a child to learn. Segregation with the sanction of law, therefore, has a tendency to retard the education and mental development of negro children and to deprive them of some of the benefits they would receive in a racially integrated school system."

Whatever may have been the extent of psychological knowledge at the time of Plessy v. Ferguson, this finding is amply supported by modern authority. Any language in Plessy v. Ferguson contrary to this finding is rejected.

We conclude that in the field of public education the doctrine of "separate but equal" has not place. Separate educational facilities are inherently unequal. Therefore, we hold that the plaintiffs and other similarly situated for whom the actions have been brought are, by reason of the segregation complained of, deprived of the equal protection of the laws guaranteed by the Fourteenth Amendment . . .

PUBLIC POLICY ANALYSIS

Public policy analysis is a regular process within government administrative operations, including district, local/county, state and national levels. The primary purpose of such analysis is to properly identify problem areas or issues, correct or resolve them, determine how much correction would cost, whom would it benefit, how many, when, and the consequences of action. Typically, an analysis results in a prioritized listing of recommendations for action, including the advantages and disadvantages of each suggested activity in the short term, long term, or both. The agreed-upon general steps of the process are called agenda building, policy formulation, policy adoption, policy implementation, and policy evaluation and assessment.

One prominent example of the process was the handling of the issue of persons with disabilities and their access/lack of access to employment in the American workplace. The problem was articulated, Congress was lobbied, the public was brought in through the media, and the issue became part of the public agenda. The end result, eventually, was the congressional passing, and presidential signing, of the Americans with Disabilities Act in 1992, and the assignment of the EEOC as the monitoring agency. The success of the process was evident when the EEOC received over 7,000 complaints of discrimination against employers during the first eleven months of the ADA's implementation.

ESSAY WRITING

The integral relationship between writing and logical reasoning cannot be overemphasized. Essay Writing is generally to persuade, explain, establish causation, entertain, infer relationships, and predict or recommend decision-making. It is a process of stating a claim or position, directly or indirectly, providing some kind of evidentiary support of that claim, and presenting it to readers to get them to see the claim the author's way. While all essay writing is not necessarily to persuade or convince, it is surely to guide or influence the thinking of whoever reads it.

Essay Writing is a logically ordered process with a beginning, middle, and end, when done effectively, with the beginning establishing the thesis (claim, purpose, position taken), the middle elaborating on it, and the end summarizing, concluding or "wrapping up" the discussion of the thesis. There are also several writing strategies commonly in use specifically associated with the intended purpose of the writing.

For example, regarding persuasive writing, using dialogue as an argument form allows an author to use a contrived Socratic yes-no format which can show alternative reasons for a particular viewpoint, provide an evaluation of opposing claims and contrary evidence, and build a gradual chain of ideas and support to a preferred conclusion. Another strategy widely used is practical reasoning, which is based on Stephen Toulmin's formulation of a programmatically reasonable approach to making claims, providing data to support those claims, and identifying commonly accepted principles to link it all together. With qualities, reservations, or limitations of the claim, and backing (the latter a set of reasons demonstrating why the principles identified are especially relevant in the case at hand), practical reasoning is normally seen as a dynamic, fluid structuring of evidence for and against claims, assumptions, probabilities, and the interrelationship of truisms, rules of conduct, or other principles which link it all together.

Other strategies include ethical, emotional, and logical appeals, and Rogerian persuasion. They're all, however, styles based on the same ordered foundation as described above.

There are numerous examples of the use of logic in essay writing within this text and within any regularly published news magazine and daily newspaper. Your English instructors would also love to show students numerous prime examples.

APPENDIX

To help familiarize beginning students with the fun and potential of logic, the following short play/skit is provided. Students can read or memorize the play for presentation in class.

WHAT'DYA MEAN, WHAT AM I SAYING?

Characters:

The Professor
The Class:

Billy	Majorie
Rafael	Justine
Serge	Miles
Cynthia	Ross
Melinda	Danielle

Class Chorus (Any number of students)

Scene: A modern college classroom. The professor is erasing the board and just getting ready to start the day's lecture.

PROFESSOR: . . . And today, we'll start our discussion of logical truth trees and derivation proofs.

BILLY: (Raising his hand, and clearing his throat so he can be heard) Ahem! Uh, Professor! Uh, before you get started today, can I ask you this question?

PROFESSOR: (Turning around) What's on your mind, Billy?

BILLY: That's just it. All these formulas and rules of logical order have fried my brain! Is all this really necessary, Professor?? I just want a good grade outta this class, and a college degree so I can get on with the American dream! What's logic got to do with any of that? . . . (Turns around to the class) Does anybody else feel me? . . .

RAFAEL: I got your back, Billy! What's up with all this stress, Professor? Why you trying to teach us logic in a non-logical world? Isn't that illogical in itself?

PROFESSOR: So, we have a little mental mutiny here eh? Did I promise you a quiz today? Are you gentle souls trying to avoid the issue of an exam?

MELINDA: Pardon me, Professor, but according to our syllabus, we don't have another exam until the far end of next week!

SERGE: Yeah. There's moratorium on F's in this class for ten days!

MAJORIE: Professor, don't pay them any mind! Some of us in here are real students! We know what you're teaching us has some socially redeeming value!

MILES: Speak for yourself, Majorie! I can't use it at the all-night service station where I work! Night people may be strange and sometimes dangerous, but logical, no way! And I sure can't use it at home. And I suppose trying to slam dunk on Serge and Ross on the basketball courts needs a syllogism, right? Ha Ha Ha!!

DANIELLE: And I suppose all you male chauvinists here think sexism and female bashing is logical?

ROSS: Hey, Professor! C-c-can we g-g-g-get your lecture sta-sta-started, please? D-d-d-don't let Da-da-danielle and Cynthia g-g-g-get started on another one the th-th-th-their po-political t-t-tantrums!

CYNTHIA: I beg your pardon!! Why is my good name being spoken in vain? I haven't bothered anyone in this class! Can't a body just mind her own business, take class notes and get smarter around here?

PROFESSOR: Well, you can all calm down! There is no quiz today. Okay? Now, in terms of truth trees . . . Yes, Billy, what is it now?

BILLY: Professor, no disrespect intended, but you never answered my question! I wasn't being facetious or rhetorical.

PROFESSOR: You mean, what good is logic?

BILLY: Yeah. In the real world.

MAJORIE: If some people would bother to study more and talk less, maybe . . .

BILLY: Girl, shut up!! You're not the professor!

DANIELLE: What makes you think her voice isn't due equal respect to yours??! Shut up, indeed!!

MAJORIE: Boy, don't you tell me to shut up!!

BILLY: Boy!!!?? . . . (Takes a deep breath) Look, I'm not talking to any of you ignorant people! What do you know?? Logic is still a foreign language in this class!

CYNTHIA: For some of us, maybe, but surely not for all of us! We do know who's passing this class and who's just tripping, Billy Moses! Without struggle, there is no progress against uncouth behavior, you know!

MILES: Why don't you all give the man a break?? He's just trying to ask a simple question! What's wrong with that?

PROFESSOR: As a matter of logical fact, nothing is wrong with it! Laura?

LAURA: Yes?

PROFESSOR: How would you define logic?

LAURA: Me!!?? . . . Well, hmmm . . . logic is ordered thinking, right? Logic is argumentation . . . Is that enough??

PROFESSOR: Justine! You want to add to that?

JUSTINE: Do I have to? . . . Let's see . . . You told us that . . . Where are those notes . . . Uh, logic is a form of critical thinking. That's right, isn't it?

PROFESSOR: Okay. Fine, for both of you. But what exactly does that mean? Billy here thinks it means little or nothing!

JUSTINE: I'm sorry, Professor. I don't care what Billy thinks period!

PROFESSOR: But that's just the point! What all of you think! Logic is an orderly way of thinking that goes a bit beyond what we feel, believe, wish, hope, and emotionally "think." Let me pose this question to all of you...Isn't logic simply a formal and informal process for solving problems and resolving dilemmas?

ROSS: I t-t-tthink not, Professor! And, s-s-since I t-t-think not, I a-a-a-am not!! (Everybody chuckles)

PROFESSOR: Only serious thinkers need answer.

MAJORIE: I hear my cue! . . . In fact, you're right, Professor! Logic *is* such a process!

MILES: Yeah, right!! But, even if it is, so what? There are many ways to solve problems in this life! And logic just doesn't seem to work with a bunch of corrupt politicians, dishonest business people, and too many fools running around on the loose! Isn't that what you said, Professor? You can't argue with a fool!

SERGE: Why have a gun that shoots only blanks? It'll only get you in trouble, and it can't protect you when you need it!

BILLY: Like I said, what's logic got to do with it all?

DANIELLE: It seems your simple question went above the small heads of my classmates, Professor! But I'm game! You want to play that question and answer thing? . . . Yes, one can say that logic is a process for solving problems!

PROFESSOR: And aren't problems and dilemmas just challenges to our abilities to reason?

CYNTHIA: Yes . . . yes, they are.

PROFESSOR: And don't such challenges act as catalysts for some level of orderly thinking, even when we are reluctant to confront those challenges?

DANIELLE: Yes, even when we get stressed out about problems, we still try to figure a way to handle them.

PROFESSOR: And even though our best thinking doesn't always equal our best and most effective ways to solve the challenges, don't we gain from the experience of trying to think through the problems?

MAJORIE: I can answer that! Yes! Yes, we do.

PROFESSOR: And isn't the gain in lessons learned part of what's necessary for maturity and for knowing better how to handle similar issues in the future?

DANIELLE: Quite so.

PROFESSOR: Then, Billy, isn't logic valuable in helping us get through life the best we can?

BILLY: Yeah. Yeah. Okay, but . . . all that sounds fallacious, Professor.

PROFESSOR: Oh really? How so?

BILLY: Sounds like equivocation! . . . You know, better thinking. Best thinking. Lessons learned. Experience gained . . .

PROFESSOR: Pretty persuasive stuff, huh?

MILES: But how can logic help me date Melinda?

SERGE: Nothing in life can help you there, fool! You ain't got a prayer! Melinda only dates good-looking guys with cash and a car, like me!

DANIELLE: And this is just another meat auction, I presume? You're selling another woman to the highest bidder? Is that what this is about?

ROSS: Da-da-Danielle! What's up wit'chew? What's your l-l-logic?!! D-d-d-Do you n-n-need a m-m-m-man or something??!!

CYNTHIA: Now why, pray tell, would something have to be wrong with her??!! You and these other fools in here seem to have the problem! Can't women have freedom of speech even now? The 19th amendment is over seventy years old, for heaven's sake, and the 14th most certainly includes all of us! Can some of you wake up to the 21st century?

DANIELLE: I assure you, Mr. Ross Porter, men are the least of my worries! My dilemma is how to stamp out rampant stupidity in college classmates.

LAURA: Professor, aren't they into rhetorical slanters and teasers now?

RAFAEL: They gonna be in the dozens in a minute here!

ROSS: I'll t-t-t . . . mmmm . . . I'll tell you what! Danielle, I cha-cha-challenge you to an ex-ex-ex-extemporaneous debate! I s-s-say Logic is m-m-m-m-more of a p-p-pain in the be-be-be-be-behind than it is a b-b-benefit! Y-y-you argue the o-o-opposite! If I lose, I'll l-l-let you tie a r-r-r-rope around my neck and dra-dra-drag me a-a-around like your love s-s-s-s-slave f-f-f-for one whole day!

MELINDA: For a whole week!

MILES: Girl, who woke you up?? . . . Go 'head, Ross! Bet her a week!!

ROSS: Nahh! I b-b-bet her one d-d-d-day with m-m-me, b-b-b-ut a week dragging your t-t-tired behind around i-i-i-if I lose!!

MILES: What . . .!! I'm not in this!! My name is Wes, and I'm not in this mess! I don't need you for no hero, Ross! But I've got your back, though! So go 'head on with your bad self!! Score some points!

DANIELLE: So, you boys want to play, is that right? Ladies!! What do you think? Should we kick some butt or what?

(A chorus of female voices, including LAURA, MELINDA, JUSTINE and CYNTHIA): Kick some butt and take some names!!

DANIELLE: Okay, here's the deal. You win, you've got your dream date! I win, then it's one week for you, and the next full week for your little pal Toto over there! And I'll bring the rope! (Sticks out her hand) Deal?

ROSS: Uh . . . hmmm . . . O-k-k-k-kay. D-d-deal!

CYNTHIA: Professor, will you please referee and keep them on point?

PROFESSOR: My pleasure. Maybe we'll find ourselves a little more logic here today after all! . . . And, let me sweeten the pot somewhat. The winner gets 15 bonus points on next week's quiz. The loser gets 5 extra points for the effort! Okay? . . . You two ready? . . . Ross, you start!

ROSS: O-k-k-kay! Just l-l-let me finish th-th-these last notes! I'm c-c-coming! . . . (Ross stands up, and strides to the front of the class. He coughs, takes a few sips of bottled water, and begins. There is no trace of his previous stuttering.)

Logic is annoying, tedious and too ponderous for modern world circumstances! In the urban environment, the public generally wants quick, fast, snap decisions and actions. The slow deliberateness of logic belies that. One has to ask whether some strongly held opinion is an argument or not, screen it through the why, what, and how, then if it is an argument, determine its validity and its soundness through its math-looking formula, whether it committed any fallacy of relevance or circular reasoning, how to handle the amorphous thing in a critique process, and all that! By the time you finish getting that all together, whoever was speaking or writing in the first place is long gone! One may arrive at a neat, orderly conclusion, but who cares?!! The object of your logic has moved on, thinking you an idiot as you stood there calculating and writing all those techniques down. No, I say! It's better to simply respond emotionally, maybe yell and scream at the opinion-maker, throw a few choice euphemisms, downplayers, or innuendoes his or her way, get in the last word and move on down the road with your bad self. The pace of the modern world demands it! Syllogisms are silly and out of place, and Sherlock Holmesian derivation proofs are a sure sign that you are unemployed, in jail, or otherwise disconnected to the modern world because you obviously have too much time on your hands! No, I say, fit in, stay tuned in, keep your wits kicked in for the quicker requirements of modern living. And if you need a logic detective, simply hire one! They are always out there on the fringes, waiting for some of us to slow down long enough to pay them some attention and maybe to give them an assignment or a job! Logic in the modern world: find you a computer geek! For the rest of us, move out of the way. We've got places to go and people to meet!! (ROSS smiles, bows to DANIELLE, and retakes his seat. The class applauds, and his supporters whistle and stomp.)

DANIELLE: My opponent appears to seek status as a thoroughly modern Willie, I see! . . . Well, to each his or her own! Let me get straight to the point! Modern informal and formal logic teaches one how to compel others to pay attention to one's point of view. People may not agree with you, but they won't be able to ignore your oral and written positions either. Logic helps you learn to write decent, orderly, coherent and persuasive essays. Techniques of logic are what A and B students regularly use. Well-learned logic gives you a decided advantage in learning how to pass, not just how to take, classroom and especially standardized exams. Logic livens up everyday conversations, and when you hold your friends accountable for what they say and challenge them to back up their points of view, well, boring it's not! My opponent said that logic is generally too deliberate and slow. Of course, it can be in the hands of deliberate, methodical personalities. But logic in the hands of the quick-witted can be devastating. The last word is most often had by those better trained in techniques of correct argumentation and evaluation. And here is my last word. Logic is not only valuable in the practical, modern world, it is also a necessary and required asset in the repertoire of winners and power-brokers! To those who are easily led and more easily duped, follow your speeding emotional responses! To those of us with our sights on making policy and deciding local, state, and national strategies and agendas—Long Live Logic!! We wouldn't leave home without it!...And lastly, to negate my opponent's need to offer a rebuttal, he presented a decent logical argument to prove to us that logic is not valuable in the modern world. Well, his very approach defeated his own purpose! In order for his argument against arguments to be taken seriously, one has to accept the validity and value of logical argumentation! . . . So, sorry Mr. Porter! No dream dates here! However, I will expect you in the Quad in front of the school tomorrow morning at 8:30 sharp for your dog collar! (The crowd laughs. There is a round of applause for both speakers.)

END OF SKIT

INDEX